ArtScroll Series®

Rabbi Nosson Scherman / Rabbi Meir Zlotowitz

General Editors

Dear Daughter

Published by

Mesorah Publications, ltd

*A father's wise
guidance for
wholesome human
relationships,
a happy
marriage and
a serene home*

by
**Rabbi Eliyohu
Goldschmidt**

**Foreword by
Rabbi Nosson
Scherman**

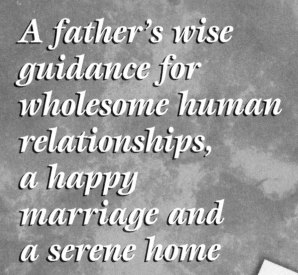

FIRST EDITION
First Impression … June 1999
Second Impression … June 1999
Third Impression … September 1999

Published and Distributed by
MESORAH PUBLICATIONS, LTD.
4401 Second Avenue / Brooklyn, N.Y 11232

Distributed in Europe by
J. LEHMANN HEBREW BOOKSELLERS
20 Cambridge Terrace
Gateshead, Tyne and Wear
England NE8 1RP

Distributed in Israel by
SIFRIATI / A. GITLER
10 Hashomer Street
Bnei Brak 51361

Distributed in Australia and New Zealand by
GOLDS BOOK & GIFT SHOP
36 William Street
Balaclava 3183, Vic., Australia

Distributed in South Africa by
KOLLEL BOOKSHOP
Shop 8A Norwood Hypermarket
Norwood 2196, Johannesburg, South Africa

ARTSCROLL SERIES®
DEAR DAUGHTER
© Copyright 1999, by MESORAH PUBLICATIONS, Ltd.
4401 Second Avenue / Brooklyn, N.Y. 11232 / (718) 921-9000

ISBN:
1-57819-288-9 (hard cover)
1-57819-289-7 (paperback)

Typography by CompuScribe at ArtScroll Studios, Ltd.
Printed in the United States of America by Noble Book Press Corp.
Bound by Sefercraft, Quality Bookbinders, Ltd., Brooklyn N.Y. 11232

Dedication

This book is dedicated to the blessed memory of my step-father-in-law, Reb Moshe (Milton) Shuster, ע"ה, a noble and sincere person who devoted his life to fulfilling the will of Hashem.

Tana d'vei Eliahu writes, "If a person resolves to be righteous and tell the truth, he is assigned an angel who escorts him and helps him speak the truth." The question arises: Our Sages have already told us that "a person is led along the path he chooses for himself." What special significance is there in the assistance a person receives when he resolves to tell the truth?

It would appear that there are two different forms of assistance a person can receive from Heaven. In general, this Divine assistance helps a person live according to his own strengths and abilities. But with regard to telling the truth, there is a particular Divine favor that raises him to a higher level.

We knew Reb Moshe, ע"ה, for 25 years, and during all that time we never ceased to marvel at his conduct. He saw the positive in every person and always stressed it. He never spoke *lashon hara* or said anything that was in any way demeaning to anyone. His words were pure and gracious, an honor to the Name of Heaven. The truth shone from every word he spoke, and it was clear that a heavenly angel walked by his side.

He loved to pray in the yeshivah and to be in the company of Torah scholars, and he imbued his values in the younger generation. He taught them how a Jewish daughter can create a home in which peace, harmony and love of Hashem reign supreme.

MAY HIS MEMORY BE A BLESSING!

Table of Contents

Foreword

In modern times, hardly a week goes by without an alarming report on the state of marriage and the nuclear family. Times were when the Orthodox community considered itself safe from such rot. The community was relatively insulated. Its values derived not from the popular media, but from the eternal values of the Torah and the traditions that were still fresh from *bubbes* and *zaides.* These traditions established the foundations of the strong family life of generations past, where the emphasis was on allegiance to God, loyalty to spouse, dedication to children, and a steadfast acceptance that values come first and creature comforts last. People were not deluded. They knew that not all marriages were outstanding successes, but they also recognized that, as a very wise, funny, and loving mother counseled her newlywed daughter, "Marriage is very hard — but you have to make it work, because we won't take you back." Everyone laughed, but the message was clear. Marriage is good — very good — but not necessarily easy. It requires effort, a very worthwhile effort, but effort nonetheless.

Many social scientists have commented that a "fast food, instant gratification" society is particularly vulnerable to family stress, because problems within the home are hardly ever amenable to "quick fix" solutions. Since Creation, people have learned to live with pain and to function well despite discomfort — whether it was a nagging cold, a nagging employer, or a nagging spouse. Whether in health or human relationships, people expected to cope, to endure, to compromise, to adjust, to give in, to grin and bear it, or sometimes just to bear it. Nowadays, there is less tolerance for inconvenience. There are antidotes for pain, insomnia, and stress. Once unpleasant annoyances have become grounds for law suits. Common nuisances are targets of legislative and regulatory attack. In such a climate it is natural to look for emotional versions of acetaminophen, ibuprofen, and aspirin to salve away the problems that invariably crop up in family life. The toleration threshold is low and seems to get lower — and if the familial discomfort persists, there is a growing inclination to escape it. If the culprit is an unsuccessful marriage, all too often the slogan is, "Marriage should not be hard. If it doesn't work, we'll take you back."

Unfortunately there are no magic potions. In a time when "values" are derided and tolerance is scarce, countless individuals and families are adrift on an uncharted sea. The results are everywhere in frightening statistics of family breakdown, youthful alienation and violence, failing schools, and opportunistic leaders.

Orthodox Jews are still far, far from the maelstrom, but they are not immune. No longer do we live in isolated *shtetls*. No longer are our homes and schools secure against pernicious influences. Double-income families and working mothers have brought the marketplace into the home. Even so-called family newspapers and magazines often have pictures and articles that could only be bought in back alleys 50 years ago. The invasive media have become such a problem that even staunch defenders of the First Amendment look for ways to limit their excesses.

The extreme dangers are well known, and sensitive families try to avoid them, but just as the most serious environmental concerns are often invisible, so too the worst enemies of husbands and wives trying to build a wholesome Jewish home are the insidious ones, the imperceptible seepage of toxic influences into Jewish families. What are they? Here are just a few: obliviousness to the ancient Jewish concept that a spouse is *bashert*, and one must be ready to accommodate oneself to him or her, the same way one adapts to one's own height, abilities, and even shortcomings; the popular style of humor that stresses insult and sarcasm; the modern addiction to gossip and dissection of personality, because there is no other way to fill so many pages and so much air time; Madison Avenue's supremely successful efforts to create demand for ever more products and fashion a culture of consumerism; the stress on money; the unwillingness to crawl into someone else's skin and try to understand what is important to the other; the culture that attacks and demeans, instead of discussing and understanding. The list is endless, but these are all among the influences that, more and more, are impinging on the Torah community and exerting strains on the family.

The need to define and beware of subtle distinctions is stressed by the Torah itself. At the end of the chapter dealing with the animals and birds that may and may not be eaten, the Torah says: *You shall distinguish between the clean animal and the unclean, between the clean bird and the unclean (Leviticus 20:25).* Quoting *Toras Kohanim (9:7), Rashi* comments that the Torah need not say that one must be able to distinguish between a cow, which is kosher, and a donkey, which is not — the difference is obvious. Rather the Torah requires us to distinguish between small but critical differences, between a slaughter that cut through a bare majority of the trachea and esophagus (which is kosher), and one which cut only half of one or both (which is unkosher). The difference is only a hairsbreadth.

Such is the case in ritual law: A hairsbreadth can make all the difference, just like in the physical world. The barest rise in the earth's average temperature can imperil human life, an engineer's slightest error can cause a bridge to buckle — and a *shochet's* failure to slice a tiny fraction of an inch can disqualify the slaughter.

And such is the case in weighing values, lifestyles, and relationships. We live in a modern world, but we must always beware of how much of modern attitudes we will permit into our minds, hearts, and children. Homes are more vulnerable than institutions, because the framework of the home rests on two people, husband and wife, not on rabbis and *roshei hayeshivah* who uphold generations of tradition. And in modern times — with their strains on livelihood and incessant pressure to conform to the images and standard of living that are imposed by influences that are usually alien, if not antagonistic, to age-old Jewish values — the barrage on marital serenity is extreme.

Rabbi Eliyohu Goldschmidt brings a lifetime of Torah learning and human understanding to bear on marriage, the family, and human relationships. Hundreds of families have come to rely on his incisive wisdom and gentle counsel. To him, husband and wife are equally precious components of the cornerstone of Jewish life: the family. Each must consider the other more than the self, the "you" more than the "I" — not merely because that is the secret of a harmonious relationship, but because that is the best way to nurture and elevate the self and the I.

As *mashgiach* (spiritual guide) of Yeshivah Zichron Moshe of South Fallsburg, and as a highly respected counselor in the yeshivah community of Lakewood, Rabbi Goldschmidt has accumulated a wealth of experience in dealing with the strains of family life. As a wise, perceptive, and sensitive Torah scholar, he knows how people relate to one another and he has developed the priceless skill of knowing what to say and how to say it.

Contrary to today's secular society, Rabbi Goldschmidt knows that the roles and psyches of men and women are different. Just as God instructed Moses at Mount Sinai to deliver the same message in different ways to the men and women (*Exodus* 19:3), Rabbi Goldschmidt speaks to men and women differently. His Hebrew work *Sechel Tov* is directed to husbands. In it he tells them what is expected of them. It echoes the messages he has delivered to them privately and in his popular lectures.

In this book, Rabbi Goldschmidt speaks to wives. Better said, he speaks to his *"Dear Daughter."* In the form of letters to his daughter, he responds to her concerns, defines her needs, and helps her shape her responses.

There is no way to do justice to the wisdom that saturates this book and the valuable and practical advice that fills its every page — other than to say it should be read and re-read, pondered and discussed by every wife and mother who seeks holiness and happiness in her marriage and family, just as *Sechel Tov* should be read by every husband and father.

Rabbi Nosson Scherman
Sivan 5759 / June 1999

Introduction

When the Chafetz Chaim got married for the second time, he was already over 70 years old. His wife was a widow in her middle 30s. When the *shidduch* with the Chafetz Chaim was proposed to her, she didn't want to hear of it. Although the Chafetz Chaim was already famous as one of the greatest people of the generation, she could not see herself marrying a man more than twice her age.

After much persuasion, however, she agreed at least to meet with the Chafetz Chaim. It was arranged that they would meet in an inn, and she was already sitting at a table when the Chafetz Chaim arrived.

He walked over to her table and sat down. He said a few words of greeting, and then he got straight to the point. "I want you to know," he said, "that I cannot offer you any more than that to which every Jewish woman is entitled according to the Shulchan Aruch."

The simplicity and directness of the Chafetz Chaim's words penetrated to her heart, and she immediately decided to marry him.

This story was told to one of the Chafetz Chaim's *talmidim* by the *Rebbetzin* herself. But I believe it requires a little explanation. What message did the Chafetz Chaim's words convey that caused such a complete change in her thinking?

Normally, when a man and woman meet to consider matrimony, it is only natural for them to try and make a good impression on each other. Accordingly, the Chafetz Chaim should have tried to impress the young widow as an energetic and vigorous man despite his age. But in actuality, the desire to make a good impression derives from self-interest.

By his one simple sentence, however, the Chafetz Chaim showed clearly that he was not focused on himself but on the needs of his prospective wife. This was his approach to marriage. "What can I do for you? Despite my limited means, I will make sure you have everything you deserve." This was the message that penetrated to the heart of the young widow and convinced her to marry a man much older than she was.

The Rashba writes in his responsa (60), "At first, Hashem considered creating man and woman as two separate beings, just as He had created the male and the female of all other species individually. But in the end, He created them as one fused being so that the woman would be taken from one of his ribs and remain as one of his limbs, 'bone of his bones, flesh of his flesh.' In this way, she would always seek to bring benefit to her husband, and her husband would seek to bring benefit to her."

This is the essence of the marriage bond, the desire of each partner to bring benefit to the other.

How is this best accomplished?

Our Sages have expressed themselves on this subject in their singular concise style, with each of their golden words full of profound and important messages. In this book, I have attempted to elucidate these messages and present practical ways in which they can be implemented.

This is not the first book I have written on the subject of *shalom bayis.* It is, however, the first I have written specifically for women. Several years ago, I published a Hebrew-language work called *Sechel Tov,* which was directed primarily to men. It was very well received, and many people asked me why I didn't write one for women as well.

Why indeed? I have to admit that I found the prospect rather daunting. First of all, in order for a book directed to women to have a reasonably wide readership it would have to be written in English rather than Hebrew. Unfortunately, English is not really my natural language. I grew up in Spanish-speaking Argentina and have spent my adult life in the hallowed walls of the yeshivah.

But there was also a more fundamental barrier. My background as a *mechanech* has been as Mashgiach of the Yeshivah of South Fallsburg. My whole experience, the trend of my thoughts, the choice of ideas and words, the form of presentation, these are all geared to young men. Speaking to women, however, is an altogether different story.

When Hashem told Moshe to give the Torah to the Jewish people, He used different expressions for women and for men. To the women, He said, *"Ko somar,* so shall you say." To the men, He said, *"Ko sagid,* so shall you tell."

Among the many explanations for this difference, a particularly fascinating one arises from Tosafos in *Gittin* (71a). Tosafos points out that *amirah*, saying, indicates the use of words, while *hagadah*, telling, can also be accomplished through other means such as sign language.

The most important element of communicating to men is simply to get the message across, regardless of whether the medium is verbal or otherwise. Women, however, relate to issues in a broad and complex manner involving both the intellect and the emotions. Therefore, it is insufficient simply to convey a message to women. It is also important to touch the emotions and the soul. Words have the power to reach the essence of a person, to inspire and uplift, whereas other means of communication such as sign language can only impart the bare message.

Clearly then, to write a book for women, especially on such a delicate subject, would require more subtle skills than I have readily available to me. Still, I felt the urgency of the matter, and I began to work on this project.

It was difficult, and I often felt myself completely in the dark. But "the people that walked in darkness have seen a great light" (*Yeshayahu* 9:1). The Midrash connects this *passuk* to learning Torah. People who enter the vast realm of the wisdom of Torah begin by walking in darkness, but the Almighty rewards their toil with a great light. In this endeavor, too, I felt that my toil was rewarded with a great light from the Almighty, which helped me find a suitable format for insights, ideas and stories, and I want to thank Him from the depths of my heart for giving me the privilege and honor of conveying the words of our *Sages* to our holy Jewish women.

Many stories, including some about *gedolim*, are woven into the letters that form the chapters of this book. They are all essentially factual, although I have taken the liberty of making minor adjustment for reasons of privacy and clarity.

I also want to point out that I have written this book to raise the consciousness of Jewish families about issues that can interfere with the peace and harmony of their homes. I do not represent the advice I give in these letters as authoritative, as the final word. I am sure others may have variations about how to achieve the ends which we all seek. Only with regard to the unequivocal prohibition against fighting in the presence of children am I willing to take an authoritative position.

⌒

Many people have offered me their kind assistance in this difficult project, and I would like to express my gratitude to all of them for their time, effort, comments and advice.

First and foremost, I would like to thank my dear wife, my *akeres habayis*. She helped me mold and attune my thoughts into a form that would be well received by women. Her keen insight and the experience she has gained over the years through contact with numerous women from a wide range of backgrounds has been invaluable. She gave generously of her time despite her duties within the house and without, and I am extremely grateful. I would also like to take this opportunity to thank her for all the years of standing beside me, both during my two decades in *kollel* and afterward, with such *mesiras nefesh* and *simchas hachaim*. May Hashem bless and reward her for her goodness.

I also want to thank my two daughters-in-law, Mrs. Lyba

Goldschmidt and Mrs. Devora Goldschmidt, for editing the early versions of the manuscript with great effort and dedication.

Special thanks to Mrs. Judi Dick, my *mechuteneste,* for her tireless efforts in guiding this work through its various stages. Her advice and many hours of reviewing and commenting on the manuscript were invaluable.

Acharon acharon chaviv, I want to thank Harav Yaakov Yosef Reinman *shlita* for his masterful revision of the manuscript, rendering it into its present form.

— 1 —

An Island
of Holiness

Dear Daughter,

I feel very honored that you and your husband should turn to me for advice on marriage and raising children. Perhaps you'll find the following story illuminating.

Last year, a young couple came to ask my advice. They had just been blessed with their first child, and they wanted to know the key to bringing him up correctly.

They were quite prepared to do anything required of them, but they wanted me to boil it down to the single most important piece of advice. In a nutshell, they wanted to know, what is the key to successful parenting?

I think they must have been taken aback by my answer.

"If you want to make sure your child grows up happy and fulfilled," I told them, "you must arrange a formal ceremony at which the two of you, your child and two fully qualified witnesses, will be present. You will then proceed to draw up a *kesubah* between yourselves and your child, which you and the witnesses will sign."

"A *kesubah*?" the young mother asked incredulously. "Like a marriage document?"

"Exactly. In the marriage *kesubah*, the husband assumes an ironclad obligation upon himself to pay a specific sum of money to his wife should he ever divorce her. In this special *Kesubah* with your child, you will both assume the most solemn commitment to provide your child with a harmonious environment and never, ever, under any circumstances, to have a fight or argument in his presence or earshot."

The young couple exchanged puzzled glances. Then the young man cleared his throat, obviously embarrassed, and said, "Well, this is like a pretty negative thing we have to avoid, and naturally, we both know it's important. But it's not exactly what we had in mind when we came here. We were sort of thinking more in terms of some positive advice about how to deal with the child. Things like that."

"Did you ever stop and think that the *kesubah* is also a pretty negative thing?" I said. "Imagine. You're standing under the fragrant, flower-bedecked *chupah*, dressed in magnificent wedding attire, surrounded by the glowing faces of family and friends. You are on the threshold of a new life, and your hearts throb with joyful anticipation. And just at this moment, we read the *kesubah* which spells out the husband's obligation in case of divorce. Divorce! Don't you think it's a little incongruous?"

"Come to think of it, it is strange," he replied. "So why do we do it?"

"Because the key to the future happiness of the couple is the sense of security. When the husband's unequivocal commitment to the future of his new bride is announced in public, she experiences a profound feeling of security, and this becomes the wellspring from which the invigorating waters of love, esteem, companionship and harmony will flow."

"I see," said the young woman. "And that must be why it's considered such an honor to read the *kesubah* under the *chupah*."

"Very clever of you," I said. "Your are quite right. Well, the same applies to your child. In order for him to blossom and develop as he should, he needs the security of growing up in a home in which peace and harmony reign supreme. Nothing can be more detrimental to a child's development than seeing discord between his parents, nothing can be more painful, more devastating to his emotional well-being. Right now, when you are looking to the future in such a positive light, this is the time to think of your child's security and make a solemn commitment never to have a dispute or speak to each other harshly in front of him. Just make sure he always sees peace and harmony between the two of you, the most important people in his life, and everything else will fall into place. That, in a nutshell, is the key to successful child-rearing."

The young couple thanked me very much and left.

I can guess what you're thinking. You're wondering if they actually went off and wrote a *kesubah* with their child, right? Well, I made sure to tell them they didn't really have to, that I was just trying to make my point very emphatically. They breathed a sigh of relief, but I could see the message had gotten through.

You know, everyone understands that *shalom bayis* is very important for the happiness of the couple, but not everyone realizes how critical it is for the well-being of the children.

This idea is actually derived from the Midrash, which states, "When a person dwells in his home in peace he will find his honor there as well." What exactly is the connection between peace and honor?

The Sages regularly use the word honor as a reference to all those worthy things that bring honor to a person. In this light, the Sages are telling us that if a person dwells in a home characterized by peace and harmony he will be able to achieve high goals in life. Just as plants need water in order to grow and flourish, a person needs a peaceful and harmonious environment to blossom and attain his full potential.

A number of years ago, I was introduced to a boy from a troubled home whom everyone considered retarded. I have to admit that he didn't make a much better impression on me. Some time later, I heard he had been evaluated by a psychiatrist — with surprising results. It seems this boy was phenomenally talented, practically a genius, but his home situation had stunted his development.

On second thought, these results were not so surprising after all. Every teacher who has experience with children from dysfunctional families will tell you how common this is.

So, my dear daughter, if you are asking my advice on bringing up your children, this is what I would tell you. If your child grows up secure in the knowledge that his parents love, respect and cherish each other, he will become a strong and confident person, well prepared to deal with the challenges life will inevitably place in his way. If your child grows up in peace and harmony and never sees signs of any sort of rift between you and your husband, he will be emotionally stable and at peace with himself. There is no greater gift you can give him than this.

Let me tell you something about my own experiences growing up in Argentina many years ago. You, my fortunate daughter, are accustomed to the way things are today for observant families in the major Jewish centers. You have friends, neighbors, schools exactly the way you want them, not to mention every conceivable kind of kosher food in every conceivable flavor. But back then in Argentina, it was vastly different world.

When I was growing up, a family such as mine, that adhered strictly to Torah and *mitzvos*, was a rarity, perhaps even less common than intermarried couples. Because of my family's observance, I faced far more restrictions and deprivations than my friends did. We did have kosher meat and one kind of kosher cheese, but beyond that, there were absolutely no kosher products available. Delicatessen did not even come into consideration.

What natural reaction would you expect from a boy in my situation? Resentment? Jealousy? Well, let me tell you, I felt nothing of the sort. It simply didn't occur to me to envy my friends who came from more permissive families in any way.

Do you know why?

Because my parents had created a home which was an island of holiness, a fortress to defend our family against the world around us. There was such peace and harmony in our home that I naturally viewed my parents as a king and queen, as our Sages say we should, and I was always immensely proud of them. My parents respected and cherished each other, and were ever sensitive to the feelings of the children. And most important, I never heard a single harsh word pass between them.

Our home was a happy, secure place, a veritable Garden of Eden.

So tell me, if you live in the Garden of Eden, are you jealous of the forbidden fruits and lax lifestyles of the children in the street?

This is my passionate plea to you, my dear daughter, on behalf of my precious grandchildren. The most important thing you can do for them is never to let them see discord in your home. Give them the greatest gift imaginable. Bring them up in a Garden of Eden.

— 2 —

Gold on the Mountaintop

Dear Daughter,

I need your help. After writing my last letter to you, an idea has begun to take root in my mind.

You are, of course, familiar with *Sechel Tov,* the *sefer* I wrote about *shalom bayis.* In that one slim volume, I discussed the obligations of a Jewish husband to his wife, as outlined by our Sages. In sixty short chapters, I explored all the aspects of the husband-wife relationship that contribute toward a happy and peaceful home.

I deliberately did not compile a manual with specific instructions, but rather, I tried to convey to the reader the spirit of the teachings of our Sages and the inspiration that can be derived from them. I would expect each individual reader to have enough common sense to apply these basic concepts to his own situation and create an atmosphere of love, companionship, harmony and peace in his home.

The response to *Sechel Tov* has been good, and I am very proud of the achievement. But the main thing is that husbands are beginning to pay more attention to their obligations to their wives. Believe me, the world can use a little more peace and quiet, a little more sweetness and light. And if I can have a small part in spreading it, I shall be very grateful.

But anytime you publish, you can expect plenty of criticism, and I've received my share. Most of the criticism stated that I had placed altogether too much emphasis on the obligations and the role of the husband, when in fact it takes two people working together to create harmony. How can I argue with that? It is absolutely correct.

So what can I do? I have been put under pressure to write a book for Jewish wives as well. But in order to reach as wide an audience as possible, it would have to be written in English and follow a different format.

I have to admit to you, dear daughter, that I was at a loss. How could I write such a book? Would I come across too stiff, too preachy? What style should I use? What kind of presentation? And yet, I felt I had no choice but to make the attempt.

But now, I've found the answer! I think I should do what comes most easily to me. I should talk to my wonderful and intelligent daughter. All the things I want to say I should write to you in letters. What do you think of that idea?

I've always felt comfortable talking to you. You are my best listener. You always hear me out patiently and ask just the right questions. So I want to take advantage of your fine qualities in writing my book for Jewish wives. If you would just take a little time to read my letters when they come and send me your comments, the book will take form by itself. I am very excited.

Please don't be offended by anything I write. The advice, my dear daughter, is not directed at you personally. You are just my sounding board as I write for the benefit of all Jewish wives. If one or another of these pieces of advice is useful to you and your husband, that would just be an added bonus for me.

Before I start, I have to warn you that some of the things our Sages expect from a Jewish wife may seem a bit extreme to you. But be patient and open-minded. Our Sages had the most profound understanding of human nature. They knew the keys to boundless love between husband and wife, and each word of their advice in this respect, as in all respects, is like a precious gem.

You must understand that if our Sages make serious demands of husband and wife, the rewards more than compensate for the effort. If someone knew that if he'd climb to the top of the mountain he'd find a pot of gold, do you think he'd hesitate for a moment? Would he worry that he might scrape his knees or bruise his elbows? Well, believe me, whoever follows the advice of our Sages in his relationship with his spouse will find a treasure worth far more than a pot of gold.

I understand, of course, that the words of our Sages may seem very distant from us at first, but we can certainly relate to them as an ideal towards which we must strive.

I am reminded of a beautiful letter I saw just recently. A group of Kollel families had gone to spend the summer in a place where the Jewish residents were far removed from anything you and I would recognize as Yiddishkeit. After one transcendent Shabbaton, a lady was inspired to write to one of the Kollel wives.

"I have some thoughts I wanted to share with you," she wrote. "After we left tonight, we stopped at a convenience store for something to drink. Mind you, this is something I do just about every day, but tonight was different. Everything seemed strange and alien to me. I saw women scantily dressed. I saw young people with rings in their noses, wearing cut-off jeans and torn sneakers. How different this scene was from the one we enjoyed together with you. Suddenly, I wanted no part of it. Not for myself. Not for my husband. Not for my children. I want what you have, the modesty, the purity, the goodness. I can't say I'm ready to turn my whole life around and live exactly as you do, but I know in which direction I'm heading. And trust me, one of these days I'm going to get there."

This letter is a very good example of how we can relate to the teachings of the Sages that may seem a little remote from us right now. They are the ideal we must seek, the direction in which we must travel.

If we embrace the teachings of the Sages, then we truly expect that one of these days we are going to get there. And when we do, the reward will be greater than any gold on a mountaintop.

Let me tell you a story. By the way, this story and all the other stories that will appear in my future letters are true, although I reserve the right to doctor them a little bit from time to time to protect the privacy of those involved or to help bring out the point I am trying to make.

Many years ago, a very great woman, the wife of one of my *rabbeim*, passed away. My friend Moshe and I made plans to go to the funeral together. As it turned out, however, Moshe left with an earlier ride, and I was to come somewhat later with his wife and her parents.

As I waited for them to leave, Moshe's wife made frantic last-minute arrangements for her small children. Her mother waited at the door.

"Come on, hurry," her mother said. "If we don't leave right away, we'll run into traffic and we'll miss the funeral."

"Yes, mother," she replied. "I'm going as fast as I can. I'll be ready in a minute. I'm almost done."

Finally, the last of the children was bundled off to a neighbor, and Moshe's wife disappeared into the kitchen.

A minute passed. Then two.

"What are you doing in there?" her mother called out nervously. "The children are taken care of. Now, let's go!"

Her daughter came rushing out of the kitchen, one hand shoved into her sleeve of her coat, the other grasping a brown paper lunch bag.

"What's that?" asked her mother.

"It's just a snack for Moshe," she said as she turned the key in the lock. She handed me the bag and asked me to give it to Moshe when I saw him. I put it in my coat pocket.

"I can't believe this!" her mother fumed as we hurried to the car. "A snack for Moshe? At a time like this, when every second counts, you have to stop to make a snack for Moshe? What is he, a little child? He's a grown man. If he is hungry, he'll find something to eat. Don't worry, he won't starve. What are you, some kind of a slave? And besides, there'll be such a big crowd there, it will be impossible to find him to give him the snack. The whole thing is so ridiculous. What a waste of time!"

Her mother continued to berate her as we got under way, but she bore it in stoic silence. Her father and I, sitting together in the front seat, spoke to each other in low tones to cover our embarrassment.

Fortunately, we did not get caught in traffic, and we arrived in time. A great crowd had turned out for the funeral, but I had no trouble finding Moshe. We sat together as our *rebbe*, a very old and feeble man, eulogized his distinguished wife with great emotion. Caught up in the pathos of the moment, I completely forgot about the snack nestled in my coat.

Later, as we settled into one of the cars going to the cemetery, I suddenly remembered. I pulled the snack from my pocket and handed it to him. "Here," I said. "Your wife sent this for you."

Moshe took the bag from me with a puzzled look on his face. He opened it up and peeked inside, and he began to cry like a baby.

"Moshe! Why are you crying I asked?" I asked. "It's just a little snack. Your wife sent you a little snack. Why are you crying?"

Moshe wiped his eyes. "You don't understand. I'm not crying for myself. I'm crying for our *rebbe*. When I saw that snack I was so touched by my wife's thoughtfulness and sensitivity. My heart was suddenly all aglow. And then I thought about our *rebbe*, that he won't ever again experience his wife's special warmth and concern for him, that he would never experience the rush of feeling I just had when I opened that little bag. How terribly sad! How could I help but cry?"

How indeed.

So who was right? Moshe's wife or her mother? In the middle of the mad rush, she forced herself to take out two minutes to show her love and concern for her husband, and look how deeply he was touched. Was it worth it? I don't think there's any question about it. Much more than a pot of gold, I would say.

$$— 3 —$$

Opposites Attract

Dear Daughter,

You have no idea how happy you have made me by agreeing to collaborate on my book. Believe me, your comments and criticisms will be very helpful. As a young wife, you are the perfect representative of the audience I am addressing, and your thoughts will surely reflect the thoughts of so many others like you.

So we begin.

Do you remember that Garden of Eden we spoke about? So how do you go about making your home into a Garden of Eden?

Naturally, it requires a little effort. If it happened by itself, every home would be a Garden of Eden and the world would be a perfect place. Clearly, it requires dedication and perseverance on the part of both husband and wife in many different aspects of the relationship.

Before we get down to specifics, I would like to address some general issues which can lead to problems and misunderstandings.

Our Sages tell us that when "a man and woman come together the *Shechinah*, the Divine Presence, rests in their midst, and if it should depart, they would be consumed by fire." Our Sages apparently felt that without the exalted residence of the Divine Presence in the Jewish home it would be impossible for husband and wife to live together in peace, harmony and companionship.

Now, I ask you, why should this be so? Think back to all those years you spent in summer camp. Didn't you have the most wonderful time with your sweet roommates? At least, that was what you always told us in your letters. So why is it so farfetched for husband and wife to get along?

How about when you went to seminary and stayed in the dormitory? You shared a room with one girl from South Africa and another from Texas, and you had the most wonderful time. Those two girls were so different from you in outlook and background, and yet you had no problem sharing a room with them for nearly a year. And although you were all very nice girls, I don't think the *Shechinah* took up residence among you. Still, you had no problems living together. Why then would it be impossible for husband and wife to live together without the stewardship of the *Shechinah*?

The answer is really quite simple. Men and women were created as total opposites — in their temperaments, their characters, their way of thinking. The differences are apparent from earliest childhood and only become more pronounced with maturity.

The Torah tells us that when Chavah, the first woman, was created Hashem said, "Let us make for [Adam] a helpmate against him." The Rishonim explain that Chavah was the exact opposite of Adam, and it was precisely this polarity that was essential for their marriage to be successful.

When you were living together with your roommates in camp and seminary, you were all basically similar, in spite of your differences, and therefore, very few problems arose. At the same time, you have to admit that living with your husband brings you more happiness than you imagined possible, far more than you gained from the companionship of your roommates.

Why is that so? Because you and your husband are opposite by nature, and each one complements the other. Together you are much more than each of you was as an individual. This is the dynamic that leads to a successful marriage.

We find these differences highlighted early in the Torah. When the angels came to visit Avraham, he told his wife Sarah to "hurry" and use coarse flour to bake bread for the guests. But Sarah, not content to serve them bread made from coarse flour, took her time until she had fine flour. Then she prepared the very best meal she was capable of producing.

The Chasam Sofer points out that these different approaches to hospitality reflect one of the fundamental differences between men and women. Men, being action-oriented, place more importance on the guests being served immediately than on the merits of the meal. "Hurry up, it's good enough" is what a man is likely to say. But women, being more passive, are natural perfectionists, and they are likely to place more importance on the guests being served well rather than quickly. This is just one of the many differences between men and women.

Hashem, in His great wisdom, designed them as exact opposites to bring diversity and balance into the marriage. It is important to keep this in mind in order to deal wisely with the irritations and misunderstandings that may arise in married life.

Some of the things that irritate wives about their husbands are just the normal expressions of the male nature. If you understand this, you will be able to deal with them calmly and constructively. After all, you wouldn't be offended if your tooth began to ache, would you? Why? Because that is just natural. Teeth sometimes ache. The same holds true for the marital relationship. The normal expressions of the male nature can sometimes cause irritation to a wife.

This is especially true about the things husbands and wives say to each other. As you know, we are all deeply affected by what is said to us. Words of praise and recognition give us profound satisfaction, while derogatory and hurtful words can wound us deeply. But sometimes, a husband's words may seem hurtful to us even though they are not meant to be. They may just be the male way of expression, and if a wife appreciates this, much friction can be avoided.

I believe I wrote you about my trip to Israel by boat many years ago and how I had to spend some time in Italy along the way. Something interesting happened on that trip, something that stuck in my mind for a long time.

During my stay in Italy, I had to arrange certain things for myself. In Argentina, where I lived, Spanish is spoken, but Spanish is not much use in Italy. Nonetheless, Spanish and Italian are related languages, and I am able to muddle my way through with Italian. As you can well imagine, I had quite a hard time communicating, and very often, I had to resort to sign language, believe it or not. But I took it all in stride and never got frustrated or upset when I couldn't get my message across.

Earlier on that same trip, we had also docked briefly in Spain, and I had gone ashore to send a letter home. Not surprisingly, I had no Spanish stamps, so I asked a person I met in the street where I could buy some. He had no idea what I was saying. Apparently, the Spanish have a different word for stamps. After a while, I gave up on asking about stamps, and instead, I asked him where I could find a post office. Another brick wall. It seems they have a different word for post office as well. By this time, I was fit to be tied. Eventually, a crew member who saw my frustration came to my rescue and helped me secure some stamps.

Sitting on the deck of the ship as we sailed through a peaceful sea on the last leg of our voyage to Israel, I found myself thinking why my language problems had affected me so adversely in Spain, yet so mildly in Italy. What was the difference?

It didn't take me long to come up with the answer. In Italy, I didn't come with high expectations because I knew I was speaking a language I didn't really know. Therefore, I wasn't frustrated when I couldn't communicate. But in Spain I expected to have no problem whatsoever, since Spanish was my language. Therefore, when I couldn't communicate I became frustrated and upset.

It is the same in marriage. If a young woman goes into a marriage with the foreknowledge that her husband has a different way of thinking, expressing himself and doing things, she will not suffer the unnecessary frustrations that can put such a strain on a marriage.

All it takes is a little wisdom and a little patience. And a little time.

— 4 —

*A Match
Made in Heaven*

Dear Daughter,

One of the surest ways to undermine a marriage is to second-guess yourself. Yet this is what many people do, especially during the early stages of marriage. When things get a little rough, they sometimes think back yearningly to others with whom they had gone out while they were dating. "Ah, if only I had married that one," they tell themselves, "I would not be having these problems."

This is a terrible thing to do, a masterpiece of the *yetzer hara* who is always seeking to sow doubts and tensions where peace and harmony reign.

What is wrong with this way of thinking? Well, obviously, it is totally counterproductive. You go and create a fantasy spouse in your mind who is a model of perfection, and then measure your real life spouse against that dream image. Is that fair? Will such fantasies help solve your problems or will it just make them worse? Besides, the chances are that you would have had some problems with anyone you marry, so this all self-delusion.

But there is a much more fundamental flaw to this way of thinking. It assumes that you had options, that you could have married this one or that one, all according to your choice. But that is not true.

Our Sages tell us in unequivocal terms that *zivugim*, matches, are made in Heaven, that each of us has a spouse who is *bashert*, preordained, just for us. Hashem, who knows the innermost secrets of every soul, matches up men and women according to His infinite wisdom, and then He manipulates events to bring these people together in marriage.

So you see, any other people you may have considered while you were dating were nothing more than illusions, false turns on your way to the goal towards which Hashem was leading you. Once you understand this and take it into your heart, your whole approach to your marriage will change.

If a king were to send two people on an important mission to a distant land and along the way these two messengers had a falling-out, what do you think would happen? Do you think they would waste time and energy squabbling with each other? I don't think so, and neither do you. In all likelihood, they would put their differences aside and find a way to work together to bring success to the king's mission.

Well, when two people get married, they must understand that they have been sent on a mission by the King of all kings. He has carefully selected these two people to work together to achieve certain goals. There are children that they have to bring into this world. There are accomplishments that are expected of them for themselves, their families, their communities. And if dis-agreements arise between them, they have to find a way to resolve them without jeopardizing the success of their mission.

You agree with me, my dear daughter, that if people thought

this way they would avoid so much unnecessary pain and heartache, don't you? So why don't they think this way? Surely, they believe the words of our Sages. Ask any religious person if they believe that matches are *bashert*, and they will assure you that they do.

So what is the problem? The problem is that they believe it in their heads but not in their hearts. They have not integrated it into their outlook as one of the facts of life. It does not have sufficient reality for them.

Let me tell you a story I heard from Rav Shneur Kotler *zt"l*, the Rosh Yeshivah of Lakewood, about his father Rav Aharon Kotler *zt"l*.

After the Second World War, Rav Aharon sent a certain rabbi on a mission to the displaced persons camps in Europe for the Vaad Hatzalah. On the way back to the United States, the plane on which he was to have returned crashed into the sea. There were no survivors. The rabbi had checked in at the flight desk, and his name appeared on the passenger list. It seemed certain that he had been on the plane and perished along with all the other passengers.

The rabbi's bereaved family called Rav Aharon and asked him how they were to observe the *Shivah* (mourning period) in this case.

"Don't sit *Shivah* yet," said Rav Aharon. "I'm sure you know the famous saying of our Sages that *sheluchei mitzvah einan nizakin*, people on a *mitzvah* mission are protected from harm. I'm telling you that, under the circumstances, there is not enough evidence to make us assume that he is dead. I personally will continue to believe he is alive until I see absolute evidence to the contrary."

The following day, the family received a telephone call from the rabbi, very much alive, telling them he had just landed. He had indeed checked in to the other flight, but he had gone off to find a *minyan* for *Minchah*. By the time he got back to the plane, it had taken off without him.

A remarkable story, isn't it? But do you know what is most remarkable about it? Not that the rabbi reappeared after he had been given up for dead. The most remarkable aspect of this story is Rav Aharon's phenomenal *emunah* in the words of the Sages. No matter how many indications there were that the rabbi had perished, the assurance of the Sages remained uppermost in Rav Aharon's mind. To him, the words of the Sages were more real than the evidence of his senses.

The Psalmist (92:3) declares, "And Your faith in the night." In our own times, we see that aircraft with sophisticated instrumentation can "see" perfectly in the darkest night. For us as well, *emunah* serves as the instrumentation with which we can penetrate the darkness that often envelops our senses.

Rav Aharon had this special instrumentation, and he demonstrated it to us by the way he lived his life. To Rav Aharon, the sayings of the Sages were not just abstract ideas. They were the facts of his life, as real to him as the sun up above and the air that he breathed.

We, too, must make the realization that matches are made in Heaven one of the facts of our lives. We know it, because our Sages told us so. We know it, because we see it all the time. How many times have we seen matches come about in ways that are nothing short of miraculous?

Now we have to take that knowledge and implant it into our hearts. We have to make it become part of our daily awareness. Every time (or at least very often) we look at our husband, we should think, "This is the man Hashem sent me as a life partner. Hashem wants me to fulfill my purpose in life with this man."

Believe me, my dear daughter, if all wives and husbands would keep this truth in mind all the time there would be no marital problems.

Let me tell you another story that I read in an article many years ago.

During the worst times for Jews under the Communists in Russia, many yeshivah students were sent to the labor camps in

Siberia for the terrible crime of learning Torah. The Soviets were not very sensitive to human rights issues, and the Jewish prisoners were all forced to work on Shabbos. Nonetheless, the captive yeshivah students tried to limit their transgression as much as possible. Whenever the guards would go on break, they would alter their work methods to avoid Shabbos desecration.

Once, the guard reappeared unexpectedly and caught on to what they were doing. The yeshivah students were all arrested for high crimes against the state, an offense that carried a possible death penalty. The trial began, and it quickly became apparent that the defendants stood no chance. A guilty verdict seemed a foregone conclusion.

During this time, a very high-ranking officer appeared in the camp. He had been passing nearby when his car broke down, and he stopped at the camp for assistance. When heard that a trial was taking place, he wanted to know all the details. Then he asked to speak with the defendants in private. In deference to his high rank, he was permitted to do so.

"Listen to me," he said to the yeshivah students when they were alone in private. "I am Jewish, just like you, but I am not observant. My father, however, was a very pious Jew. On his deathbed, he made me give him my word that I would always be kind to other Jews. Well, coming here and hearing what's going on, I got the feeling that this was one of those situation that called for some kindness to my fellow Jews. So this is what we're going to do. You people are going to make some very convincing apologies, and I'll prevail on the camp commandant to accept them."

The officer was as good as his word, and the prisoners were reprieved.

Years later, while in the United States and reminiscing about his Siberian experiences, one of the former prisoners made an interesting observation.

"Until that miracle saved us," he said, "life in the Siberian labor camp was just about unbearable. We could not bear to live from one minute to the next, so terrible were our conditions. But once we saw Hashem's hand, through the miraculous appearance of that officer, reach down into the camps to save us, everything changed. Suddenly all those hardship were no longer so unbearable, because we were constantly uplifted by the knowledge that Hashem was with us every moment of every day."

This is a very important point. When a person knows Hashem is with him, guiding him every step of the way, he finds it much easier to deal with the annoyances of life. This applies to everything, financial problems, health problems and certainly marital problems.

Knowledge and acceptance of Hashem's guiding hand are critical to happiness and success in life.

You know, I'm reminded of a telephone conversation I had with a friend last summer. I was speaking from the comfort of my home, but he was in a bungalow in the mountains. I remember him complaining about the unending rains that had forced him to be "cooped up" in his bungalow for an entire week.

"Look at it this way," I consoled him. "Rain is a wonderful blessing."

"Of course, it's a blessing," he said. "But a whole week? C'mon! Enough is enough!"

Ridiculous, isn't it? What does this man know about rain? What does he know about the ecological cycles of the world? And yet, he has decided that a week of rain is too much. Why? Because it doesn't suit his personal plans!

So what's my point? Very simple. Hashem has chosen a spouse for each of us according to His infinite wisdom. He knows why this particular spouse is the perfect match for us, and we have to accept it with profound faith and trust.

We have to accept it as a fact, a given in our lives. This is my husband. This is my wife. The one that was meant for me. The one Hashem chose for me. No one else could have possibly taken the place of my spouse.

Someone once said that a spouse is like a missing tooth. You think that's strange? I don't blame you. It is a bit strange.

This piece of special wisdom derives from an anecdote. A man was mugged in a park on his wedding day. One of his front teeth was knocked out, and he suffered assorted other bumps and bruises. In desperation, he ran to the dentist for a replacement tooth.

On short notice, however, the dentist could not do a great deal. He took some of the teeth he had in stock and tried cutting and trimming them to make them fit. But try as he might, none fit perfectly.

Suddenly, the dentist had a brainstorm. "Why don't you go back to the park and see if you can find the tooth that was knocked out?"

The man returned to the park, and sure enough, he found the missing tooth. It was caked with blood and dirt, but still intact.

The dentist cleaned it and sterilized it. Then he inserted it into the gap. It fit perfectly.

The same holds true for a spouse The one Hashem has chosen for you fits perfectly. No one else does.

Dear Daughter,

As always, I can expect you to reply with sharpness and insight, and you have not disappointed me.

If Hashem has already chosen your husband well in advance of your meeting, what is the point of all the effort parents put into *shidduchim*? Why make so many telephone calls and try so hard to find out information when it's all out of your hands anyway?

That is an excellent question.

All I can say is that finding a *shidduch* is like making a living. We all know that, no matter how hard we try, our success or failure is entirely in Hashem's hands. And yet, we are required to make our own *hishtadlus*, a reasonable effort to earn a living. If we make the *hishtadlus*, then Hashem gives us whatever He has decided to give us. The connection between the *hishtadlus* and the *berachah* is the subject of much philosophical discussion, which we can talk about some other time, if you wish. But we all understand and accept that this is so.

The same applies to finding a *shidduch*. We are required to make our *hishtadlus*, a reasonable effort to find the right spouse. But in the end, everything comes solely and entirely from Hashem.

When Hashem brought you into this world, He provided everything you would need here. He provided you with lungs, kidneys, a heart, a brain that are the perfect match for you. He also provided you with the husband who is the perfect match for you. And He brought the two of you together under the *chupah* and set you off on your holy mission of building a faithful house among the Jewish people.

Your match was made in Heaven. What the two of you make of it is up to you.

But I can promise you this. If you really take the words of our Sages deep into your heart, if you truly believe with all your being that your match was by Hashem in Heaven, you will surely make something very beautiful and holy out of it.

⌒

Dear Daughter,

One last word on the subject.

An old uncle of mine used to say that marriage is like a pair of shoes. When you buy a new pair of shoes, they look so shiny and elegant, but when you put them on, they pinch a little. No matter how perfect the fit, the shoes will not be entirely comfortable for a while. But once you break them in, they are so comfortable that you cannot imagine being without them.

The same holds true for marriage. No matter how perfect the "fit," there will inevitably be minor irritations and discomfort in the beginning until the couple are fully adjusted to each other. But once that happens, marriage is a supremely comfortable state.

There is, however, a very important condition.

Let's go back to the analogy of the shoes. If a person buys a pair of shoes, he fully expects them to pinch him for a while, and he is prepared to tolerate it until they are broken in.

But what if he bought the shoes at a clearance sale because they were the last pair left and he is not sure if they are exactly his size? Would he have the same confidence that the pinch is only a temporary nuisance?

Not likely.

So what will he do?

He'll try to stretch the shoes and twist them this way and that to make them fit better. And in the process, he will ruin the shoes.

When will he have the patience to wait for the pinch to go away? When he was fitted by an expert and feels confident that these shoes are exactly his size. Only then will he feel sure that the shoes are essentially comfortable and that the pinch will soon disappear.

The exact same holds true for a marriage. If a person is not confident that his spouse is the perfect match for him, he will not be so content to tolerate the minor difficulties of the adjustment period. Instead, he will try to stretch the marriage this way and that until he can actually ruin it.

But if he is confident in the assurance of our Sages that his spouse is the perfect fit for him, he will find the patience and perseverance to get through the adjustment period with grace and humor. Then he will discover the incredible comfort that the marriage will bring him, and he will forever thank Hashem for a match that was clearly made in Heaven.

— 5 —

Awakening the Roots

Dear Daughter,

Before I start on the next topic, let me tell you a story I heard when I was still living in Argentina. In Montevideo, the capital city of our neighbor Uruguay, there lived a Jewish couple. Let's give them names for the sake of the story. How about Jorge and Myriam Zimmerman?

Well, Jorge and Myriam were quite happy for the first few years of their marriage, but then they began to have problems. It started with small things which don't even bear mention. Then they ran into financial difficulties, and the little rift in their relationship grew into a gaping chasm. One thing led to another, and before long, there was uninterrupted war in the Zimmerman household. Jorge and Myriam couldn't even say a civil word to each other.

They decided to divorce.

They made all the arrangements with a rabbi, and then they made an appointment with an attorney to finalize the financial settlement.

As she was getting ready to go to the attorney's office, Myriam was listening to the evening news on the radio. Suddenly, there was a flash bulletin. There had been a massive explosion in a gas main downtown, and there were casualties. Preliminary reports mentioned a few names of the victims. Among the dead was one Jorge Zimmerman.

Myriam could not believe her ears. Her heart fluttering wildly, she spun the dial to find other stations carrying the news. Perhaps she had made a mistake. But she hadn't. As the bulletins kept coming in, the name of Jorge Zimmerman kept coming up on the list of confirmed dead.

Myriam began to cry hysterically. She thought back to her wedding day and all the happy times she had enjoyed with her husband. And now he was dead! How could it be? Even worse, he had died in the midst of terrible marital strife, his life blighted by misery and despair.

Consumed by grief and guilt, she barely heard the telephone ring. Finally, it penetrated her consciousness, and she picked it up.

"Hello, Mrs. Zimmerman," said the attorney. "You are late for your appointment."

She burst into tears once again. "What are you talking about? Didn't you hear the terrible news? My husband is dead. There was an explosion downtown, and he was killed. Oh, Heaven help me!"

"Mrs. Zimmerman, I'm sorry to disappoint you," he replied, "but your husband is sitting here with me right this minute. We're both waiting for you to come. And you're late. Here, talk to him yourself."

As soon as Myriam heard her husband's voice, she fainted.

When she regained consciousness, she was a changed person. All her resentments and accusations had vanished into thin air, swept away by the relief and the love that had been reawakened in her heart by the shock of his reported death. It did not take long for Jorge to respond in kind, and the Zimmermans resumed their marriage successfully. If anything, it was now more blissful than it had ever been.

People are always moved by this story. It's very romantic. But what does this story really tell you?

Let me tell you what I think.

If you ever cut your finger, do you go into a panic? Of course not. You know perfectly well that your body will heal itself. The blood will clot, and the bleeding will stop. New repair tissue will be generated to replace the damaged tissue, and in a short time, your finger will be as good as new.

Well, Jewish marriages also have the ability to generate repair tissue. It is only to be expected that your marriage will suffer little nicks and scratches from the strains and pressures of daily life. But under normal circumstances, there should not be any permanent damage. Your marriage will generate its emotional repair tissue, and before long, it will be as good as new.

So what happened to Myriam Zimmerman? She allowed the minor irritations of marriage to undermine her feelings for her husband. She went from love to irritation to disgust to outright hatred. And so all the little things were blown up out of proportion until there seemed to be no other option than to separate and divorce.

By not facing reality, she had constructed a living hell for herself. True, it would have been a sugar-coated living hell, with comforts and friends and a social life. But in the final analysis, it would have been a life of loneliness and despair. And if Hashem had not shocked her back to her senses, she would have taken the fateful step and broken with her husband.

So how did the shock of thinking her husband had been killed turn her life around? Why didn't all the minor irritations reappear once the shock had worn off?

The answer goes to the heart of the matter. The roots of the love between husband and wife are very deep, and as long as they function well, they are constantly regenerating repair tissue which wipes away those minor scratches without a trace.

But sometimes those roots of love are numbed by anger and resentment. Then they stop producing repair tissue, and all the minor scratches begin to fester and throb until they become intolerable.

When Myriam Zimmerman suffered her shock, the deep roots of her love for her husband were reawakened. Suddenly, new repair tissue was generated, and all those emotional little nicks and bruises vanished.

This is the essential lesson that Myriam Zimmerman's experience teaches us. If only the deep roots of love between husband and wife can be awakened, most irritations and annoyances will simply disappear. In His infinite wisdom, Hashem has arranged a Jewish wife to resume the role of a bride to a certain extent every month of the year. Through this blessing the roots of love are constantly reawakened and renewed, and there is an endless flow of repair tissue to bring the marriage back to its perfect condition despite the stresses of everyday life.

So you see, my dear daughter, if you make it your business to approach every single month with the enthusiasm and excitement you felt on your wedding day, to reawaken the roots of love and give them new vitality and vigor, yours will be a truly blissful marriage.

Let me bring this point out just a little better with an analogy. You know we have a custom of the father blessing the children every Friday night. Why is the reason for this custom? Do you know?

I once heard that it is to provide a moment of reconciliation. During the week, responsible parents have to be strict with their children, to restrict their pleasures and to discipline them occasionally. Although they have the best intentions, it is almost inevitable that parents will hurt the feelings of their children from time to time.

According to the Torah, if you hurt someone's feelings you must seek his forgiveness. Therefore, we bless the children each Friday night. During that moment, when the child stands bathed in the holy glow of the candles and the serenity of the Shabbos home, he feels his father's hands settle gently on his head under the smiling gaze of his mother, and he knows that his parents love him with all their hearts. That special moment erases any irritations that may have arisen between parent and child and returns their relationship to perfect purity.

Your monthly reunion with your husband needs to be in the same spirit. Forget the squabbles and the inconsequential frictions, and recreate the holy atmosphere of your wedding day, with the innocence and fluttering hearts of a young groom and bride. As the *Shevet Mussar* advises, the Jewish wife should declare, "My husband, I love you eternally!"

Awaken the deep roots of love in your marriage, and you will surely be blessed with peace, harmony and everlasting happiness.

— 6 —

The Best in the House

Dear Daughter,

You may have heard this story before, but I don't think you heard my interpretation. So bear with me.

The Midrash tells the story of a couple who were married for ten years and were still childless. The husband wanted to give his wife a divorce so that he could remarry and have children. And so they went to Rabban Gamliel and asked his guidance.

Rabban Gamliel listened to them carefully, then he nodded. "Yes, I think you should get divorced. But since you are doing this for the best of reasons, because you want to have children, I do not want you to treat this as an ordinary divorce. Instead, I want you to have a private celebration at home, just as you had a celebration when you were first married."

They went home and prepared a beautiful feast just for the two of them.

During the meal, the husband drank a lot of wine and became somewhat intoxicated. "My dear, you know I hold you in the highest regard," he said expansively. "I want you to have all that your heart desires. Tonight, when you return to your father's house, take whatever you want with you. Take the best in the house. It is yours."

Having finished his little speech, the husband nodded off and was soon fast asleep.

The wife called for her servants and ordered then to pick up her husband and carry him to her father's house.

Hours later, the man awoke, bewildered.

"Where am I?" he asked his wife.

"You are in my father's house," she replied.

"But how did I get here? And why?"

His wife smiled sweetly. "Well, do you remember telling me that I should choose the best in the house and take it with me?"

"Yes, I do. But I still don't understand."

"It's you, my dear husband. You are the best in the house. There is nothing I want or like better in the entire house than you. Therefore, following your instructions, I had my servants carry you to my father's house."

The man was deeply moved by what his wife had done and said. And he didn't know what to do.

The next day, they returned to Rabban Gamliel and told him what happened.

Rabban Gamliel told them to go home together and forget about the divorce. All would be well. Then he prayed for them, and they were blessed with a child.

A beautiful story, isn't it? But it is not so easily understood. Rabban Gamliel had a boundless love for every single Jewish soul. Why then did he first advise the couple to divorce? Why didn't he immediately send them home with the assurance that he would pray for them to have a child?

Not so simple, eh?

Well, let me tell you what I think, but first I must tell you another story.

Rav Isser Zalman Meltzer, the Rosh Yeshivah of Slutsk, was married to Rebbetzin Baila Hinda.

When Baila Hinda was 16 years old, a famous *gadol* had visited her home, and her father asked him to give the young girl a blessing.

"What would you like, my child?" asked the *gadol*.

"I would like to marry a man who will be a great Torah leader of the Jewish people," she said.

"Indeed?" he replied, his eyebrows raised in incredulity. "Only a great Torah leader you want? Nothing less would suit you?"

The girl burst into tears. "Yes, yes, that is all I want," she sobbed.

The *gadol* was visibly moved by her reaction. "Don't cry, my child," he said. "I see that you care very deeply about the Torah and that you wish this with all your heart. Then let it be so. May Hashem bless you and send you a husband who will be a great Torah leader of the Jewish people."

And thus, Baila Hinda eventually married Rav Isser Zalman Meltzer, one of the *gedolei hador*.

So what exactly happened here?

Let me explain it to you.

At first, the *gadol* thought that Baila Hinda want to marry a *gadol hador* because it was a glamorous thing, not because she really wanted to dedicate every moment of her life to the Torah and the service of Hashem. After all, it could be such a nice thing. Think of it. So much honor, so much glory. And so much merit, of course. But that was not sufficient reason for him to give her such a blessing.

But when she burst into tears, he saw how true and pure her intentions really were. He saw that to her this was a necessity of paramount importance. This then was a girl who really deserved to marry a *gadol hador*, and therefore, he gladly gave her his blessing.

That is exactly what Rabban Gamliel had in mind. He was not prepared to intercede in Heaven for this childless couple unless the survival of the marriage was of critical importance to them. But when he saw the reaction of the wife, who considered nothing better in her life than her husband, he knew he had to move heaven and earth to save the marriage.

You know, it reminds me of my tonsil operation when I was a little boy in Argentina.

I can hear you laughing, right? My tonsil operation? What does that have to do with anything? Well, let me explain.

When I was a child, we very rarely had ice cream. It was a rare treat reserved for special occasions, and even then, I was allowed only a little bit. But after I had my tonsils taken out, I was allowed to have as much ice cream as I wanted.

"Why are you letting me have so much ice cream," I asked my mother, "when you hardly ever let me have any at all?"

"Ice cream is a luxury," she replied, "and we can't afford many luxuries. But after surgery, it is very important that your throat is constantly cooled and soothed. Right now, ice cream is a necessity for you, not a luxury. Necessities we can, *Baruch Hashem*, manage quite nicely."

So, my dear daughter, do your father's tonsils have anything to do with Rabban Gamliel's prayers?

There is an important lesson here for every marriage. Rashi explains that the Jewish people enjoy special blessings for love, peace, brotherhood and companionship. But when we ask for these special blessings, let us ask ourselves the following question: Why do we need them? Are they a luxury? Or are they indeed a necessity?

After all, a woman may think, "I want love and harmony in my marriage so that I can mold for myself the kind of life I want without interference from my husband. Love and harmony certainly make for a more enjoyable life." This woman is clearly asking for luxury, and therefore, her prayers are less likely to be answered.

But another woman may think, "I want love and harmony in my marriage, because my husband is more precious to me than the air I breathe, because I care more for my husband than anything else in the world, because he is the best in the house." For this woman it is clearly a necessity, and her prayers are more likely to be answered.

Think about this, my dear daughter, when you pray for yourself and your husband. Acknowledge to Hashem how much your husband means to you, and take upon yourself not to speak harshly to him, not even to think negative thoughts about him. Then you will surely deserve the wonderful blessings of unlimited love in your marriage, where pleasing each other will bring you both the greatest joy.

Dear Daughter,

In my last letter, we talked about how important it is for a Jewish woman to feel that her husband is an absolute necessity in her life. But what if a woman doesn't feel quite that way? What is she supposed to do?

Well, let me tell you another one of my little stories. When I first came to the Lakewood Yeshivah many years ago, people still used to get handwritten letters by mail. Today, a telephone call is nothing, no matter the distance. And E-mail! But then it was different. Letters were still the main mode of communication from a distance.

In the yeshivah, there was a table designated for mail. The letters were sorted alphabetically and laid out for the boys to collect. I noticed that several boys were always the first to check the mail and grab their letters with especial eagerness. Being new in the yeshivah, I didn't know from where these boys were, but I felt certain they were from overseas. It turned out I was right.

Why did I think they were from overseas? Very simple. All of the boys certainly loved their parents, but sometimes the feeling is not necessarily a burning flame in their hearts. But when they are very far away from home, they miss their parents so terribly that their love ignites into a great flame. And so these boys from overseas couldn't wait to get their hands on the letters from home and read the loving words of their parents. Did these boys from overseas love their parents any more than the others? Of course not. It was the distance between them that stoked the fires of their love.

The same holds true in marriage. Every Jewish woman who stands under the *chupah* in purity and holiness has a profound love for her husband, but the fires of this love must be stoked in order for it to burst into a great flame.

So how do we stoke the fires of love?

For a Jewish woman, the answer is through prayer.

The Shelah encourages a woman to pray daily for her husband to succeed in his endeavors and her children to progress in Torah and *mitzvos*. But at least once a week, I believe she should also concentrate on strengthening the bond between herself and her husband so that they become as one, united, inseparable.

Perhaps during candle lighting would be the most appropriate time for such a prayer. It is a time when you are exalted, standing in your own *Beis Hamikdash*, like a *Kohein Gadol* lighting the golden *Menorah*. It is a very emotional time when you beseech Hashem for all the things that are important in your life — your parents, your husband, your children. This seems to me the most appropriate time to offer up prayers that will strengthen your *shalom bayis*.

In the prayer after candle lighting, you ask for "great blessings." What are "great blessings"? Some people may think these refer to material comforts and other worldly rewards. But they are mistaken. The Shabbos candles are the symbols of *shalom bayis*, and it therefore stands to reason that the "great blessings" you ask for at this time also refers to *shalom bayis*, which is the greatest blessing.

So in order to help you formulate your thoughts and feelings a little better when you pray for this great blessing, I have formulated a short prayer which goes as follows:

רבונו של עולם אודך על כי נוראות נפליתי. נפלאים מעשיך, ונפשי יודעת מאד אשר התקנת לי בעלי לבנין עדי עד.

אנא המלך הטוב והמטיב לכל, תשפיע מטובך עלי ותנה אותי לחן ולחסד לפני בעלי, כי אהבתיו, ותשרה בינינו אהבה אחוה שלום ורעות. אנא חזק אותי ואזהר תמיד מלדבר דברי מחלוקת וכעס לבעלי, ולא אחשוב שום רעה עליו.

"Master of the Universe, I give thanks to you for the awesome and wondrous way in which I was formed. My soul knows full well that You provided me a husband with whom to build an edifice that would endure forever. O good and all-benevolent King, I beg You shower me with Your goodness and help me find favor with my husband, for I love him. Let there be love, brotherhood, peace and companionship between us. Please give me strength so that I may always be careful not to speak angry or harsh words to my husband, nor to think any hostile thoughts about him."

Think about these words, my dear daughter. Give them your own meanings and flavor and add more of your own if you want to.

When you say, "Let there be love, brotherhood, peace and companionship between us," think about the wonderful blessing of having a home which is always full of joy. How do you achieve this? By asking Hashem to "give me strength so that I may always be careful not to speak angry or harsh words to my husband, nor to think any hostile thoughts about him."

As the gateways to Shabbos open wide and the pure and holy serenity descends upon your home, as the glowing candles illuminate your home, your family, your world, pray that Hashem will ignite and preserve in your heart a flame of burning love for your husband so that your happiness will endure forever.

— 7 —

The Greatest Gift on Earth

Dear Daughter,

You know, my dear child, from time to time I think back to one of the happiest days of my life, your wedding day. I can still visualize you in my mind's eye dressed in your gleaming white gown. How utterly exquisite you looked on that night, radiant with natural beauty and grace. Yours is that special beauty of the Jewish woman, a beauty which glows with the purity and goodness within. I remember thinking how lucky your *chasan* must feel, how thankful to Hashem for giving him such a lovely bride to light up his life.

On that night, you were a princess, and your husband was a prince. But what happened after that night? Did you both go back to being common people? Was your brush with royalty just temporary, a fantasy played out for one fairy-tale night? Perhaps that is the way it is for most people in the world. But not for Jewish people.

According to the Talmud, all Jewish people are princes and princesses, deserving of all the privileges of royalty. That is the way you must always appear in the eyes of your husband, as a lovely princess. He must always think of you as the greatest gift on earth. You must always remain his princess.

So what does that mean? Should you wear your wedding gown every day? Of course not (pardon my little joke).

I'm sure you've heard of the Shelah, a very great Kabbalist who lived several centuries ago. He writes, "[The Jewish woman] should always dress up for [her husband] with humility, grace and modesty, and her garments should always be spotless." The literal translation of the word he uses, *mekushetes*, is adorned.

This is the key. She doesn't have to wear a dazzling white gown. She should dress according to the occasion, but always with the intent to please her husband, as a princess always seeks to please her prince. No matter what the situation, she should always try to look her best.

Let me remind you of something I noticed during your engagement. You were sitting at home on the couch reading a book, graceful, well groomed and very put together, as you always are.

Then the telephone rang. It was your *chasan* letting you know that he was on his way over.

Instantly, you sprang into action. Gone was that calm and radiant young woman reading serenely on the couch. Suddenly, you seemed on the verge of panic. Where was that dress? Where did you put your make-up?

"But what's the matter?" I asked, genuinely puzzled. "You look perfectly fine. More than fine. Great."

"You don't understand," you called to me over your shoulder as you disappeared into your room. "He is coming in a few minutes, and I have to look my best."

My dear child, I admit that at first I didn't understand. But when I thought it over, your words made perfect sense. For your *chasan*, good is not good enough. Great is not good enough. Only the best.

Well, the same holds true for your husband, only more so. When you hear your husband coming, don't say to yourself, "Oh, it's only him," and continue as before. Think! Is your appearance the best it could possibly be? If it isn't, do something about it quickly, before he comes. Never forget that he is your prince and you are his princess.

I know what you're thinking. Correct me if I'm wrong, as I'm sure you will. You think that this all applies to an ordinary husband. But what if a woman is married to a *talmid chacham*, a man who lives in a spiritual world and is immersed in Torah study? Does such a man also need that his wife dress up for him all the time? It is a fair question.

Well, let's look into the Midrash for the answer. Who was the greatest *talmid chacham* that ever lived? Who reached the highest pinnacles of holiness, far beyond anything we can even conceive? It was Moshe Rabbeinu. The Midrash tells us that his wife Tzipporah was a great beauty and that she used to adorn herself for her husband.

Do we need any more proof than this? Anything our Sages teach us about Moshe Rabbeinu and Tzipporah takes place on the most exalted levels of *kedushah* , holiness. Therefore, if they tell us that Tzipporah dressed up for Moshe Rabbeinu, this was an expression of the holiness that characterized every aspect of their lives. Following their example, therefore, can only raise the level of holiness in our own lives. When a woman dresses up for her husband so that he will admire her purity and beauty, she literally glows with *kedushah*, the kind of *kedushah* that brings inner satisfaction and happiness into the home.

Let me finish with one more story from the Talmud.

Abba Chalafta was a very great *tzaddik* who used to labor long hours in the fields to provide a few scraps of food for his hungry children. During a severe drought, the Sages decided to seek out Abba Chalafta and ask him to pray for rain.

In the course of their fascinating encounter with Abba Chalafta, the Sages observed many rather unusual practices, and at the end of the day, they asked him for explanations. One unusual practice was that his wife, all dressed up, came to greet him as he returned from the fields.

"Why was your wife dressed up?" they asked.

"To prevent me from looking at other women," Abba Chalafta replied.

Now let us try to recreate the scene in Abba Chalafta's house that evening before he returned home. House is surely an overly generous description. Hut or hovel would be more appropriate. The small children are playing on the dirt floor. There is no furniture except for a few broken chairs and a rough-hewn table. Piles of straw serve as bedding.

The lady of the house has her hands full. She must stretch a handful of coarse flour into enough bread to take the edge off her children's hunger. But first she must go out and chop some wood for the fire. It does not even cross her mind to hire help to do these chores. There is simply no money. While the bread, if you can call it that, is baking, she is spinning wool to make patches for her little daughter's tattered dress.

Suddenly, she looks up and glances out the window. The sun is beginning to set. Quickly, she puts down her work and gets dressed up. After a final inspection of her attire, she heads out the door.

Where is she going? She is on her way to the edge of the village to greet her husband coming back from the fields. Why? Because she doesn't want her husband, the venerable Abba Chalafta whose prayers can bring rain when all else has failed, to look at strange women.

Do you remember what you felt that day when your *chasan* called to say he was coming right over? Well. this fine lady felt it every day. And believe me, despite the hardships and poverty, this was one happy lady. And she had one happy husband.

Dear Daughter,

Your reaction to the story of Abba Chalafta's wife is only natural. You draw a very reasonable distinction between a young *kallah* who gets excited when she hears her *chasan* is coming and a mature married woman burdened with the responsibilities of running a household. You feel it's impractical and unnecessary to go to such lengths after you're married.

I don't agree.

Let put it to you this way. Jewish marriage is based on the concept of *yichud*, which means that the two partners love each other with all their hearts, souls and resources until they become as one. In order for such a marriage to be successful, each partner must be completely and totally focused on the other. The slightest thought in a man's mind about another woman, or a lingering gaze, attacks the foundations of the Jewish home.

You have to understand, my dear child, that men are very different from women. Men, by their very nature, are always seeking variety and novelty, while women are more content to stay where they are, as long as they are happy. The Torah acknowledges this difference by strictly forbidding men to look at other women. No such prohibition applies to women. You may have difficulty relating to this difference because it is beyond your personal experience, but that is nonetheless the way it is. Men and women are not the same.

You know, of course, that according to the Torah a man is exempt from military duty during the first year of his married life. The Torah makes this provision so that husband and wife will become so closely bonded that all others will seem like strangers to them.

But what happens after that first year, the idyllic *shanah rishonah*? Do you think everything will go on indefinitely of its own momentum in the same manner? Unfortunately, life does not work that way. Unless that feeling of utter closeness is constantly nourished and nurtured, it will eventually fade, like a car running out of gas.

It is your responsibility to keep your husband focused on you, to notice you and be attracted to you. Remember the peculiarities of the male nature. Your husband goes out into the world and he inevitably sees women who are elegantly dressed, well groomed and presentable. Then he comes home to you. If you make the effort to dress up for him, he will focus on your grace and beauty, and those other women will not lodge in his mind. But if you are disheveled and untidy when he comes home, he will not take notice of you and those images of other women will linger in his mind. You don't want that to happen. Believe me.

What does it take to draw your husband's attention away from the women he encounters in the outside world, to keep him focused exclusively on you? A little of your Jewish beauty is what it takes.

The Torah tells us that Sarah was as beautiful at age 20 as at age 7. Now, you know as well as I do that the gentile world considers a 20-year-old woman more beautiful than a 7-year-old girl. But not according to the Torah. Jewish beauty derives from the inner purity which shines out so brightly from the face of a young child. It is composed of not only grace but also of humility and modesty, if you remember the words of the Shelah I quoted in my last letter. But don't forget, the humility and the modesty are all good and well, but you need the grace as well. And you need it every day.

I recently visited a doctor friend of mine, and he was talking about his mother who had come to visit him from overseas. One day, she came to see him in the hospital while he was preparing for surgery. Although he was already dressed in his baggy scrubs, when he heard that his mother was there, he went out to see her for a few minutes.

She took one look at him and recoiled.

"I'm shocked at you," she said. "Such a famous doctor shouldn't wear clothes like that. There's a limit to being casual, you know."

The doctor laughed. "There aren't clothes, Mother," he said. "They're a work uniform. They are solely for function and not at all for appearance. I would never wear these things in my office when I see patients."

Do you see what I'm driving at? It's fine to dress casually at home. You can't be expected to dress up as if you're going to a wedding. But there is a limit to being casual. Once you cross the line between casual clothes and a work uniform you are in dangerous territory.

It all gets down to how you view your husband. If you give him at least the consideration a doctor gives his patients, you will always make sure he sees you neat and clean and graciously attired. All it requires is that special feminine touch and a desire to appear attractive to your husband. Just that little touch will win your husband's everlasting admiration and thereby bring untold happiness into your marriage and your home.

Dear Daughter,

I'm glad to see that I've gotten through to you, and that you've come around to Abba Chalafta's wife's way of thinking. But your questions really put me on the spot. How can I tell you what kind of clothes or how much make-up to wear?

Let me tell you a story about the Chafetz Chaim. An owner of a big factory once came to him for a *berachah*. They conversed for a while, and the Chafetz Chaim began to suspect that the man's Shabbos observance left much to be desired.

"Tell me," said the Chafetz Chaim, "do you keep your factory open on Shabbos?"

"I'm sorry to say this, Rabbi," the man replied, "but I do. I don't want to, of course, but I have no choice. Expenses are so high, and if I'd close my factory for one day, I would surely go bankrupt."

"There is no excuse," said the Chafetz Chaim. "You must keep Shabbos."

"I'll tell you what, Rabbi," said the man. "You are very wise. You explain to me how I can avoid going bankrupt, and I'll close my factory on Shabbos."

The Chafetz Chaim shook his head. "I'll do something better. I'll explain to you how important Shabbos is. Once you understand that, you yourself will figure out how to make sure that your factory stays closed."

A nice story? It's one of my favorites.

That is the answer to your question, my dear daughter. I have explained to you how important, indeed how critical it is for a Jewish woman always to appear attractive to her husband.

What exactly does that entail? You are a clever young woman, and you will figure out the answer for yourself.

Let me just make one more point regarding this subject. It may help you form the guidelines that will work for you.

Do you know why it is customary for the *kallah* to circle her *chasan* seven times under the *chupah*?

Our Sages tell us that a man without a wife is like a city without a wall. Just as a wall protects the city, so does a wife protect her husband against the temptations of the world. When the *kallah* walks around her *chasan* seven times, she is expressing her obligation to build a wall around him every single day of the week, a wall that will protect him in holiness and bind him to her forever.

What kind of wall does a city need for its protection? There is no one answer to this question. A city in a valley needs one type of wall, while a city on a rocky mountaintop needs another.

Just as there are different kinds of cities, there are also different kinds of men. One man may need one kind of wall, while another may need an altogether different kind. And no one knows better than his wife which one he needs.

My child, when you walked around your *chasan* under the *chupah*, you laid the foundations of the wall that would protect him and help him reach his full potential, both as an individual and as your husband and the father of your children. But this is not the type of wall that you can build and then walk away in the knowledge that you are safe and secure. The world tears at this wall every single day, chipping away at it little by little until, before you know it, it can disappear completely if you neglect it.

Building this wall is a lifelong commitment. You must lay another brick on this wall each day if you expect it to remain strong. And if you do, both you and your husband will reap the rewards, and he will surely look upon you as the greatest gift on earth.

— 8 —

With Loving Care

Dear Daughter,

There is an old chassidic tale about a *rebbe* in a small village who would often disappear from sight for several hours at a time.

The people in the town used to taunt the *rebbe's* followers, asking them, "Where is your *rebbe?"*

"Our holy *rebbe* is in Heaven," the *chassidim* would answer.

The people would laugh and go on their way.

One man was overcome by curiosity and decided he had to find out where the *rebbe* actually went for those few hours. For several days, he hid in the bushes behind the *rebbe's* house and waited patiently. Soon the *rebbe* emerged and walked briskly away. The man followed from afar.

The *rebbe* glanced around to see if anyone was observing him, and then he slipped into the forest. He came to a small clearing, took a small axe from under his coat and began to chop wood. After accumulating a sizable pile of firewood, he tied it into bundles and slung them onto his shoulder. Then he returned to the village and furtively deposited the wood outside the huts of the poorest families in the village. Only then did he go home.

Overawed, the man who had followed him walked slowly away. As he strolled down the street, deep in thought, he heard someone ask a *chassid* mockingly, "Where is your *rebbe*? He seems to have disappeared again."

"Don't you know?" said the *chassid*, "My *rebbe* is in Heaven."

"No, you are wrong," said the man who had followed the *rebbe* into the forest. "Your *rebbe* is in a place much higher than Heaven."

A very charming story, isn't it? And it has a very powerful message. A person who helps others is in a place much higher than Heaven. Beautiful. Helping others is not a burden. It is a wonderful achievement, a high privilege which transports you to a place higher than Heaven. I told this story in *Sechel Tov*, my Hebrew *sefer*, to encourage men to help their wives with the housework when they are needed. After all, with whom is it more important to do *chessed* than with one's own wife? But there is also a very specific message here for the Jewish wife.

Helping her husband is one of the fundamental roles of a Jewish wife. The Torah tells us, "It is no good for a man to be alone. I will make him a helpmate." And so Hashem made the woman.

How is a woman a helpmate to her husband? Our Sages understood it very practically. A man brings wheat from the field, they explained, and his wife grinds it into flour and bakes bread for him. A man brings flax from the field, and his wife spins it into thread and weaves him a garment.

So how do we relate to this in modern times? No one is grinding wheat or spinning flax these days. Ready-to-use bread and garments are easily available everywhere. In our homes, we have the most advanced appliances and conveniences to lighten the load of the homemaker, who is probably contributing to the household as a secondary, if not primary, breadwinner.

Before I try to answer this question, let me look a little more closely at the words of the Sages. Why was a woman created? To help her husband by making bread out of his wheat. Doesn't this seem strange? Why was a woman, who is so totally different from a man, needed for this job? Wouldn't another man have been just as capable? After all, in the army, men perform all these tasks, and they do a pretty good job of it.

Do you know what I think? I'm sure you do, and you are probably right.

The woman's role in the house is not that of a servant. The Torah did not assign her the task of helping her husband in order to make sure there was bread on his table. Most men are perfectly capable and resourceful enough to take care of themselves. But all men need emotional support, as do all women, and the role of the wife as a domestic helpmate is primarily to give him that support.

As our Sages say, "To stand him on his feet and light up his eyes." No space age, high-tech appliance can light up a man's eyes. When a wife cooks and bakes for her husband, he feels loved.

Our Sages say, "The greatness of drinking is that it brings hearts together." This thought is echoed in an old popular saying that "the way to a man's heart is through his stomach." I believe this is true. Cooking for your husband is one of the most eloquent ways you can tell him that you love him. It is one of the most effective ways to light up his life. Make him happy, and you will be happy, too.

The Shelah advises the Jewish wife to "serve him his meals on time and make him his favorite delicacies." Believe me, if you do this you will nourish his heart far more than you will nourish his stomach.

When I was a youngster, my mother, may she rest in peace, used to make a certain dish for me, because she knew how much I liked it. It took much time and effort to make the concoction, but she always did it gladly.

In later years, she grew feeble and had difficulty breathing, but she still made this dish for me whenever I came to her house. I often begged her to make something simpler, but it was to no avail. No matter how difficult it was, she insisted on making that particular dish. Why? Because that dish was her expression of motherly love for me.

I want you to know, that dish was a delight to my taste buds, but my mother's love, its most important ingredient, I can still taste in my heart to this very day.

Don't think for a moment, my dear daughter, that this is a one-way street. Don't think I expect you to serve your husband hand and foot while he sits back like a king on his throne. In *Sechel Tov*, I made strong demands on men to show their love and high regard for their wives. But wives don't need their husbands to bake cakes for them to feel loved. They need other things.

Recently, my friend's wife went to Israel by herself for a niece's wedding. She told her husband and children not to worry. She would be back as soon as she could. They should make do until she returned and would be able to get everything back into ship-shape order.

When she returned, she fully expected the house would look as if it was hit by a small hurricane, but she didn't mind in the least. The little extra work was well worth the opportunity to be with her family in Israel for the wedding.

When she stepped into the house, however, she was stunned. The kitchen sparkled, the floors and windows gleamed, and there was a large bouquet of flowers on the dining room table. The woman burst into tears. Tears of happiness, of course. Her husband and children couldn't have sent her a louder message of love if they had stood on a mountaintop and screamed it at the top of their lungs.

There are many ways for a man to show love for his wife just as there are many ways for a woman to show love for her husband. To a man, that delicious cake or bowl of hot soup might send the same message of love as the sparkling home did to the wife.

The key is to show thoughtfulness. The greater the thoughtfulness, the greater the love shown.

We learn this from Hashem. When He sent the *mann* down from the heavens to the Jewish people in the desert, He sandwiched it between thin layers of dew. Why did He do this? To show His consideration for the feelings of the people.

I remember that there was a box of brand-new, unwrapped soaps near the washroom in the yeshivah. Someone had taken off the wrappers so that the boys wouldn't have to bother with them. But you know what? Some boys would go into the storeroom to get wrapped soaps before they washed up. Why? Because people have the impression that something wrapped is fresher and better. In deference to this feeling, Hashem sent down the *mann* wrapped in dew. It was a thoughtful touch to show us that He loved us.

You, too, can show your thoughtfulness to your husband by what you serve him. In this way, you will be expressing your profound love and esteem for him. It is well worth the effort.

***

Dear Daughter,

In my last letter, we discussed the importance of serving your husband his favorite foods. In this letter, I would like to address housework.

By the way, I hope you notice that I say "we discussed" rather than "I wrote about." When I write to you, I can practically hear your comments in my mind, and I respond to them. So to me, this is very much a two-way discussion.

Let me tell you an interesting story I recently read in a *sefer*. There was a certain *tzaddik* in Jerusalem who was famous for learning Torah without interruption. Only the most dire emergency could pull him away from his Gemara.

A childless couple came to seek the advice of this *tzaddik* on how to deal with their marital problems. Afterwards, the situation in their home improved drastically, and they lived together in peace for many years.

After the *tzaddik* passed away, however, the troubles started all over again. What had happened? Some time later, the facts of the case came to light. It seems that the fundamental problem between husband and wife was the issue of neatness. The wife seemed to be an indifferent housekeeper, while the husband was meticulous about neatness and order.

So how did the *tzaddik* deal with this problem? He used to go to their home every afternoon when there was no one home and straighten up the house. They didn't lock doors in Jerusalem in those days, and he had no trouble getting in. The husband thought his wife was keeping the house neat, and the wife thought her husband was doing it. And so they lived together in peace. Until the *tzaddik* passed away, that is. With no one to pick up after them, the problems returned. Since *shalom bayis* was at stake, this *tzaddik* apparently considered the husband's need to have a neat home so important that he gave up his own precious learning time for it. A woman should never underestimate the importance of neatness to some men. If her husband cares very much about it, she can't just brush it aside.

The last time I was in Israel, I was asked to meet with a couple who had serious marital problems. The husband was a general in the Israeli army, and he expected military standards of neatness and orderliness in his home. His American wife had an entirely opposite attitude. The husband was so upset that he wouldn't even rule out divorce as a solution. He could not envision himself living indefinitely under such conditions.

"I think it's all ridiculous," his wife said when it was her turn. "This is a home, not an army barracks. Things are used, children play. It is only normal for it to be a little messy. Like having a chicken bone on your plate when you're eating chicken. Should you run to the garbage with every chicken bone that appears on your plate? My husband's demands are crazy, I tell you. What does he want? That my children and I should stand at attention and salute when he comes into the house? This is a home, not the army!"

I heard her loud and clear, as I'm sure you do, too. I can hear you cheering her on as you sit and read this. Well, so what would you do? Would you let this marriage fall apart?

We discussed their problems at length, and then it was my turn to talk.

"You know, you remind me of a girl I know back in America, the daughter of friends of mine," I said. "For years, she used to complain about how difficult it was for her to breathe. My friends took her to many doctors, but none of them could find anything wrong with her. They concluded that her problems were psychological, that she was just seeking more attention. Finally, they took her to a certain specialist who discovered that a tiny hole in her heart was causing her breathing difficulties."

They were fascinated by the story, but I could tell they didn't quite see the connection to their situation. "How do you think this girl felt all those years?" I continued. "Here she was having real trouble breathing and everyone thought she was just an attention-seeking complainer.

"I think the same think applies to your husband. The need for neatness is a very deep part of his emotional make-up. It is as important to him as the air he breathes. You know, it's very possible that this character trait of his drew him to a career in the army, rather than the other way around. Neatness and order is of critical importance to him. To his way of thinking, a messy home is not a home at all. Therefore, it followed that if if his wife didn't keep the house neat for him she didn't love him.

"You have to be understanding of your husband," I concluded. "If you tell him he is being ridiculous he will feel like that girl who couldn't breathe because of a hole in her heart while everyone accused her of complaining to get attention." As soon as I said these words, I saw the light of understanding appear in her eyes. From that point on, we concentrated on finding a practical solution that would satisfy everyone's needs, and you know what? We did!

Sensitivity and understanding. Sensitivity and understanding. That is what a successful marriage is all about. You must listen carefully to your husband to ascertain his needs, and he must listen to you to ascertain yours. Then you will find a way to work it out. If Hashem brought husband and wife together, there is undoubtedly a way to make it work and work beautifully. If you only look for it with open eyes and an open mind, you will find it. Without question.

✑

Dear Daughter,

You ask me how to respond to women of your acquaintance who are unhappy with their roles as Jewish homemakers. Unfortunately, this is a common problem. Many women are disgruntled with their duties at home. They feel stifled and unfulfilled, as though they are wasting their lives away cleaning up after their children. What do you tell them? This is what I would suggest.

Suppose a woman complains about diapering her children. She has to soil her hands, and she is unhappy doing it. Ask her to imagine that she is a prominent urologist or proctologist in one of the top hospitals in New York or Boston. No matter how much they try to protect their hands with gloves, they get dirty all the time. If she were in their position, would she feel as unhappy about getting her hands dirty? I think not.

So what is the difference between her position and theirs?

Very simple. They see themselves as doing something very important. And they are! They are taking care of the health of their patients, perhaps even saving their lives. So what's a little dirt on your hands when you're doing great things?

Well, let me tell you that a Jewish mother is doing something even more important. She is bringing up her children to be *talmidei chachamim* and *neshei chayil*. She is ensuring the future of the Jewish people, and she should be thrilled and inspired..

People complain because they do not value what they do.

When a friend or acquaintance expresses her dissatisfaction to you, explain to her that there is nothing more important in the world than giving her children the care and love they need in their formative years.

Explain to her that nothing is more important than showing her husband how much she loves him and cares about him.

Explain to her that nothing is more important than creating a Garden of Eden in her home, an island of serenity, harmony, holiness and pure happiness in a mad world.

Explain to her that if she would only appreciate the greatness of what she was doing, her happiness and fulfillment would be without bounds.

— *9* —

The Prince
of Your Dreams

Dear Daughter,

About 30 years ago, a government accreditation team visited Beth Medrash Govoha in Lakewood. The head of the delegation was a professor of Oriental languages who had some limited knowledge of Hebrew and the Talmud. Nonetheless, everyone knew that for him stepping into the yeshivah would be like entering another world. The lifestyle, the system, the study methods were all so different from anything he had ever experienced, and we were all curious to see his reaction.

Do you know what impressed him most about the yeshivah? It was the respect.

When the *Rosh Yeshivah* walked into the *beis midrash*, every one of the hundreds of *talmidim* in attendance rose to his feet and remained standing in respectful silence until the *Rosh Yeshivah* reached his place.

The professor had never seen anything like it in his life.

Why did this impress him more than the exalted lifestyle of the yeshivah community? Surely, they measured up very favorably against the dissolute and promiscuous students that populated the college campuses.

This is what I think. Undoubtedly, he was impressed by the pure and holy lifestyle, but he did not relate to it personally. He was as impressed as a tourist seeing the pyramids in Egypt for the first time. The respect, however, was a totally different matter. He was a professor, an educator, always wanting to share his knowledge with his students, and he surely had discovered how difficult getting through to students could be. Here he had seen a phenomenal thing. He had seen the profound respect these young *talmidei chachamim* felt for their Rosh Yeshivah, and he knew that a wide-open channel of learning connected them. This to him was truly awe inspiring.

The same holds true when there is true respect between husband and wife. It open a wide channel of love and companionship which can bring them both unlimited happiness and joy.

Very often, young men have come to me to discuss the chapter I wrote in *Sechel Tov* about the ways in which a man should respect his wife. These young men were very deeply impressed by the teachings of our Sages regarding respect for a wife. But even more important, they were excited by the possibilities that opened up before them. It was like a whole new world.

I would like you to enjoy that same excitement when you realize how important and exalted it is to respect your husband. But I would like to explain it to you in the context of an experience I had on one of my periodic visits to my parents in Buenos Aires.

While there, a young man who was very active in outreach programs asked me to address a group of secular intellectual women. It was a very important meeting, and he wanted to make an impression on them. I did not have much time to prepare, but considering the situation, I couldn't decline the invitation. I decided to begin with a quote from the Rambam.

The Rambam writes in the Laws of Matrimony (15:20), "And the Sages also instructed that a man should honor his wife . . . And [the Sages] also instructed the woman to honor her husband exceedingly, to stand in awe of him and do everything according to his direction. She should regard him as a prince or a king, acquiescing to his desires and avoiding anything he dislikes. This is the way of holy and pure Jewish men and women in marriage."

Before I could elaborate on the words of the Rambam, one of the women interrupted me. "Rabbi, this is the 20th century," she said. "Women today are well educated and as capable of earning a good living as men are. We've broken out of the stereotype of the Middle Ages. Just look around at the women here today. Professionals, businesswomen, educators. I'm sure I speak for all of us when I say I find it personally offensive to be told I must be my husband's maid. Prince or king, indeed! What am I supposed to do when he comes home at night? Throw myself on the floor and bow down to him?"

You can imagine the response that got, the laughter, the comments.

I waited till the room quieted down before I continued.

"Do any of you know why I am here in Argentina?" I said. "I come regularly to visit my elderly parents, and this is one of those times. Now, I myself am already a grandfather, but do you know how I feel about my parents? I'll tell you. When I leave Argentina to return home, I always write a thank-you letter to my parents on the plane. In this letter, I thank my parents for everything they have ever done for me, and I thank the Almighty for having given me the wonderful gift of my parents' love. And invariably, as I write this letter, I cry real tears. Do you know why I cry?"

The room was now utterly silent. I could see I had their total attention.

"Do you know why I cry? Because the laws of Judaism have implanted the deepest feelings of love and respect in my heart.

"Jewish law commands us to look up to our parents as a king and a queen. All parents, without exception. Now, it would be easier to understand this if the father and mother are brilliant and accomplished people. But what if someone has simple, unlearned, poor parents? How is he to look up to them as a king and queen?

"Our Sages tells us that even the simplest parents shower their children with boundless gifts. They start by giving them the priceless gift of life, and throughout life they proceed to shower them with innumerable gifts and kindness. It would be impossible for a child ever to repay the debt of gratitude he owes to his parents. Therefore, our Sages gave us numerous laws regarding the respect we must show our parents. These practices, performed in the spirit of gratitude and reciprocated love, inspire the child of even the simplest parents with such admiration and adoration that they truly become as a king and queen in his eyes.

"Because of the wonderful teaching of our Sages, I still enjoy that exalted feeling of happiness in the home of my parents, even though I am now a grandfather."

The room was absolutely quiet, but the emotional tension was high. I had touched a deep nerve.

"There is different model of parent-child relationships in the modern world," I continued. "A neighbor of mine, a very progressive lady, came to visit us with her daughter. After chatting for a while, the daughter turned to her mother and said, 'Susan, your neighbors are really lovely!'

"I was shocked to hear a daughter address her mother by name. It violates everything I was taught about respecting parents. But tell me this. Do you think this daughter will ever be in awe of her mother? Will she tremble at the privilege of visiting her mother? Will she feel exalted and uplifted when she steps across the threshold of her mother's house? This daughter may have gained a friend, but she lost a mother."

I could see that I had struck home. My audience was rapt.

"So now, let's see how all this relates to the husband-wife relationship. Do any of you remember the days of your engagement?"

This question was greeted with gentle laughter and broad smiles.

"Let me tell you about my daughter during her engagement. Whatever her groom wanted, she was off and running to give it to him even before the words were entirely out of his mouth. I don't think any king ever got better treatment. And do you think he was the world's most brilliant and handsome young man? No. He was just a fine young man, but the Creator has instilled in every woman's heart a feeling of love and adoration for her mate. But will it last? Will she feel the same way 10 years later? Twenty? Thirty? Aha! That depends on her. If she follows the teachings of our Sages she will keep that feeling alive and ensure that her marriage will remain eternally blissful."

The woman who had first interrupted me rose to her feet. "Rabbi," she said softly, "could you read us the words of the Rambam again?"

⸺

Dear Daughter,

That was quite a story in my last letter, wasn't it? It is amazing how powerful the words of our Sages can be if they are explained properly.

I would like to add to it a little bit now. There are certain things I can say to you which I couldn't say to them. They simply would not have understood.

There is an important *rav* in New York I visit from time to time. His wife, the *rebbetzin*, treats him with great respect. She will come in and say, "Does the *rav* want his medicine now?" I really admire her for addressing her husband in public in such a formal manner. But I once heard her talking to him through an open door, and she addressed him as Avrumie. In public, she helps maintain the respect due him, but in private she allows herself to be more familiar. This is perfectly fine.

Now let us look into the Torah. After the angels come to tell Avraham and Sarah that they would have a child in their old age, Sarah thinks, "After I have withered shall I become rejuvenated? And my lord is also old."

Sarah is in the privacy of her own thoughts, with no one listening to her but Hashem. And yet, she refers to her husband as "my lord." Now this is respect!

I want to conclude with just one more observation about how respect for your husband can bring so many benefits to your marriage. But first let me tell you another of my little stories.

A friend of mine recently took a job as a fundraiser for a well-known institution. I had advised him against taking the job, because I didn't think he had the necessary skills. But he didn't take my advice, and to my astonishment, he was a phenomenal success. It was beyond me how he could get people to give large donations, but that was exactly what he did with amazing regularity.

One day, I met one of his colleagues and asked him if he knew the secret of my friend's success.

"It's very simple," he told me. "When he visits a potential donor, he treats him as if he were among the richest people in America, ready to give millions to all good causes. The donor is so flattered and uplifted by this approach that he usually responds with a sizable donation."

The same holds true in your marriage, my dear daughter. If you treat your husband with great respect, as if he were indeed a king, he will most likely respond in the most positive way. His self-esteem will rise dramatically. Any hardship he had during his day, any slights or indignities he may have suffered at hands of other people will all disappear like the morning mist. And he will be so grateful to you that he will be ready to do anything to please you.

You will then discover that your own wonderful words have earned you the prince of your dreams.

$$— 10 —$$

Embracing
New Customs

Dear Daughter,

Many years ago, when I was still a *bachur* in yeshivah, I spent a Shabbos in the home of a chassidic *rebbe*. Although he was not one of the famous *rebbes*, his was a true chassidic court.

Among the many guests at the *rebbe's* table was an extremely intelligent German Jewish professor who displayed an encyclopedic knowledge of the Torah and an insatiable curiosity about his surroundings.

The professor had moved from Frankfurt to Australia before the Second World War. He was now in the process of writing a book about the chassidic lifestyle, and his research had brought him to the United States and the *rebbe's* table. The *rebbe* and the *rebbetzin* answered all the professor's questions very patiently, offering explanations here and there about practices and customs which must have seemed strange to him.

On Shabbos morning, the *rebbetzin* served the professor *cholent*. When she saw him look quizzically at the dish, she said, "This is like a *Bohnensuppe*." A *Bohnensuppe* is a bean soup German Jews traditionally eat on Shabbos morning.

The professor's eyes opened wide. "You said that with a perfect German accent, *rebbetzin*," he said. "How do you know such a good German? And how do you know about *Bohnensuppe*?"

The *rebbetzin* smiled. "Why shouldn't I speak a good German? I am a seventh-generation German Jew, and my parents always had *Bohnensuppe* on Shabbos."

After the meal, I went for a walk with the professor.

"I am so impressed with the *rebbetzin*." he told me. "She is a really righteous woman."

"Does being a German Jew make her righteous?" I joked.

"Young man, when I first met the *rebbetzin* I was sure she was a seventh-generation descendant of an old chassidic family, not a seventh-generation German Jew. But she actually had the same upbringing I did, which is so different from the chassidic way. And yet, she adapted herself so perfectly to her husband's ways and customs. This is truly a righteous woman of the highest order."

"Yes," I said. "I see what you mean."

"Do you know what the Meiri writes?" he continued. "The righteous woman exchanges her father's customs and ways for those of her husband until it appears she was raised in her husband's household, not her father's. Young man, the *rebbetzin* could easily pass for the daughter of a *rebbe*, even though she is a German Jew. What a righteous woman!"

This, my dear daughter, is a difficult adjustment for a good Jewish daughter. She has grown up revering the customs of her father's house. They formed such an integral part of the texture of her life. And now, she must take on her husband's customs, which may sometimes be very different from her own.

Do you know why this is such an important issue?

Let me explain it to you.

Over hundreds of years, diverse customs have developed in different circles, different communities, different parts of the world. These customs are very precious to us, and our Sages have commanded us to be as strict in their observance as in our observance of the laws, if not more so. Customs are what connect us to our ancestors and our tradition. They give tremendous stability and texture to our religious life. If you were to choose specific examples of the beautiful Jewish observances you experienced in your father's house, many of them would undoubtedly be customs.

And yet, there is no right way or wrong way in customs. Beyond the basic requirements of Halachah, there are many different ways of serving Hashem, all of them beautiful and legitimate. Each person is required to serve Hashem in the manner he learned in his father's house.

Inevitably, some people may have stricter practices in some areas while others may be stricter in other areas. This is perfectly fine, as long as they are both faithfully following their own legitimate customs.

But there is a danger here. Unsophisticated people whose customs are stricter may look down on those who do not follow these customs. For instance, many groups have a custom not to eat *gebrokts* on Pesach. No *kneidlach*, no *matzah* in the soup. They go to great lengths to make sure that not a drop of water touches the *matzah* even after it is fully baked.

Now, are the people who don't have this custom less devoted to Hashem, less *frum*? Just because they enjoy delicious *kneidlach* in their soup during the *Seder*, does that mean that they are less diligent in their observance of the prohibition of *chametz*?

Of course not. People who eat *gebrokts* are not one iota less *frum* than those who don't. Both are observing the hallowed customs of their respective communities. That is the main thing.

I once read a story about a great *tzaddik* who was extremely strict about *gebrokts*. Not a single crumb of *matzah* was allowed to come anywhere close to a drop of liquid.

One time, a man from a different community was a guest at the *tzaddik's* table on Pesach. The man was unaware of the custom of *gebrokts*, and he cheerfully started crumbling *matzah* into his soup.

The man's actions were greeted by a chorus of horrified gasps from around the table. The man looked around in confusion, mortified that he had offended his hosts but not knowing what he had done.

The *tzaddik* immediately set the man's mind at ease. He explained the custom of *gebrokts* to his guest and reassured him with many kind words. The halachah forbidding the humiliation of an innocent Jew, he explained, was far more important than the observance of any custom.

This was a very important lesson to all the people gathered around the *tzaddik's* table, and it should also be a very important lesson to all of us.

Now let's take a look at what happens if this problem crops up in a marriage. It could be disastrous.

So let us imagine for a moment that you came from a family that didn't eat *gebrokts* while your husband came from a family that did. How do you think your husband would feel if you looked down at him because, in your eyes, he is insufficiently strict in avoiding *chametz*? Or what if your husband's *posek* has more lenient opinions than the people who taught you? How would he feel if you looked down at him because of it? Not very good, I would say. Wouldn't you? And even if you said nothing, he would surely see the disdain and contempt in your eyes. Believe me, the damage to the relationship would be dreadful. And would it be worth it? Certainly not. *Shalom bayis* is more important than any custom.

So you see, my dear child, there is only one solid solution to this problem. They are the words of the Meiri I mentioned before.

"A woman must embrace the customs and ways of her husband until it appears that she was raised in her husband's household." Her acceptance of her husband's customs must be total, not only on the outside but also on the inside.

The observance of our holy Torah should bring husband and wife together, not drive them apart.

Think into this, and you will see how wise and true are the words of our holy Sages. Follow them without question, and they will bring untold happiness to you and to your entire household.

— 11 —

A Sympathetic Ear

Dear Daughter,

Last week, a *bachur* came to discuss some of his personal problems with me. Seeing that he was very tense, I suggested we go for a walk. It was beautiful outside. The sun shone brightly, and there was just the slightest nip in the air.

We walked along in silence for a while. Then he began to talk.

For the next hour, we walked and talked. Or to be more precise, we walked, and he talked. Occasionally, I would contribute a sympathetic grunt or a word of understanding. Such as, "I see." Or, "*Oy vey!*"

By the end of the hour, he was animated, even ebullient. He thanked me for all my help and complimented me for being a "master *mashgiach*." Then he hurried away to join his friends.

I stared after him for a while, shaking my head. Amazing! Believe me, I had said nothing to him. I didn't give him a single piece of advice. And yet he felt his problems were solved.

Who had solved them? He had, himself.

So what had I done for him? Why did he call me a "master *mashgiach*"?

I listened.

That's all I did. But apparently, it was enough.

Our Sages say, *"Daagah belev ish yesichenah l'acherim.* If a man has a worry in his heart, he should confide it to others." We all have a strong need to express our worries and concerns to others. Knowing that someone is listening to us with a sympathetic ear gives us a sense of relief and comfort. Once we have that emotional support, we are usually better able than anyone else to find the solutions. After all, who knows the problem better than we do?

When we are young children growing up, our parents are our most sympathetic ears. They love us and care about us more than anyone else in the world, and they hear us out with the most warmth and concern.

When we get married, we look to our spouses for that emotional support. What a wonderful feeling it is for a woman to pour out her heart to her husband, to discuss all her problems and express all her inner fears to that special someone who cares so deeply about her. And what a wonderful feeling it is for her husband as well to serve as that sympathetic ear for his wife, to give her comfort and reassurance.

This is one of the fundamental elements of the bond between husband and wife. When it is exercised, the bond becomes stronger. When it is not, the bond weakens. My dear child, never hold back from confiding your worries to your husband. Sharing and solving your problems, both big and little, is what brings you close together. Keeping your problems from each other drives you apart and damages your relationship.

But you must always use your special wisdom when you are

telling your problems to your husband. As with everything else in life, it must be done in moderation. Give him too much, and you risk overloading him and turning him off. The Torah tells us, "The voice of Hashem comes with force." Our Sages explain that the voice of Hashem comes with the amount of force that each person is capable of absorbing, even a pregnant woman. Hashem wants each of us to hear His voice. Therefore, He modulated it for each individual person to the exact level that he or she can tolerate.

I know you always enjoy my little stories, or at least you say you do, so let me tell you another one.

I was once visiting another city, and in the morning, I went to a *shul* in the neighborhood for *Shacharis*. After *Shacharis*, as my host and I were getting our coats, I suddenly heard piercing screams. I ran to the door to see what was happening.

An old man was sitting on a folding chair. He was holding his *tallis* bag and rocking back and forth crying uncontrollably. Rivers of tears streamed down his face. My heart wept for him, although I didn't know what was causing his pain.

But then I noticed something that shocked me even more. People were coming out of the *shul* and walking right by the man without giving him a second look. How could it be? How could people be so callous?

Just then my host came out.

"Do you know why that man is crying?" I asked him. "Who is he? And why does everyone ignore him?"

"It is a very sad story," my host replied. "This man is a Holocaust survivor. He saw his entire family slaughtered in front of his eyes. Every single day after *Shacharis*, he sits on that chair and weeps over his family. The people aren't ignoring him. They're just used to it. And what are they supposed to do?"

Do you hear those words, my dear daughter?

They're just used to it. And what are they supposed to do?

When people hear someone crying very often and are really incapable of doing anything about it, they just turn off.

There comes a point where the tears no longer arouse their compassion, and they respond with indifference. It is human nature.

Husbands also react according to the rules of human nature. If you overload his circuits and swamp him with worries and problems that he is incapable of handling, and if you do this often, he will inevitably shut off that wonderful sympathetic ear of his and become like those people from the *shul* walking right past the weeping man. And this would be a very bad thing, both for you and for your husband. The lines of communication must be kept wide open in order for your relationship to flourish and deepen all the time. So that is why I was saying that you should use your special wisdom to decide what, when and how you should tell him your problems. I'm not saying you should hold anything back from him. But perhaps it is not necessary to give it to him all at once.

Try to tell him your problems as calmly as possible, because if you get emotional or hysterical it puts tremendous pressure on him. He may feel incapable of dealing with you in that condition, although he very much wants to, and he will become frustrated. This, too, may lead him to turn off. Remember the modulation of Hashem's voice? You must modulate yours as well so that your husband will be able to tolerate it and give you the emotional support you need.

A while ago, a young man came to me for advice. He was having problems at home, and he wanted some help. For the most part, he was complaining about his wife, but even as he spoke, I could see that a great deal of the fault lay with him. He was clearly far too impatient with her.

I gave him a copy of *Sechel Tov* and pointed out a number of the chapters in which I explained the obligation of a husband to be patient with his wife. The young fellow, who really meant well, was excited with the book. He really wanted to do the right thing, and he promised to read the chapters very carefully.

A month later, he came to me again and told me he had read the chapters and found them very illuminating. Then we spoke about the home situation, and it was apparent that there had been very little practical improvement, if any.

I asked to meet with his wife.

After speaking with her for a half hour, I finally understood the root cause of the problem. Simply put, she expected far too much from him, far more than he was capable of giving her. And when she did not get what she wanted, she became resentful. He was constantly becoming more and more frustrated, and she was constantly becoming more and more resentful. Where was this marriage heading?

Not to a good place.

I explained to her very diplomatically that she could not make such heavy demands on her husband, that she had to be like a teacher who knew how much to demand from a student. Demand too much and you get nothing. The message got through, and I'm happy to say the situation is vastly improved.

This is a very important lesson to remember. Know the limits of your husband's tolerance. Listening to you with a sympathetic ear is as important to him as it is to you.

He wants to listen to you. He wants to give you emotional support. He wants to offer you any practical help he can. It makes him feel that he is important in your life, and nothing gives him more pleasure than making you happy and bringing you comfort. Share with him the troubles in your heart. But remember, as long as you give it to him little by little, in amounts he can handle, he will always respond with the love and caring you need for your emotional support.

— 12 —

Simple Misunderstandings

Dear Daughter,

Do you remember Yasha, the boy from Leningrad who used to come to us for Shabbos from time to time? He has been doing extremely well in yeshivah, and he seems on his way to becoming a truly outstanding *talmid chacham*. If you remember, he is such an intelligent and interesting person, a really charismatic personality.

Well, the time has come for Yasha to think about getting married, and he has been going out for several months now. But without success so far. He needs an idealistic Bais Yaakov girl who will help him reach his great potential, but it's not easy. There are such differences in upbringing and background between a Russian boy and an American girl.

Two weeks ago, I helped arrange a date for him with a very good girl. The next day, he called to tell me how it went. He was very excited. Then he began to tell me in detail about the conversations. One of the things he had chosen to speak about really caught me by surprise.

"Yasha, I can't believe it," I said. "You brought that up on a first date?"

"Actually, I did," he said. "She is very intelligent girl. So cultural differences between us not make problem. We had good, open conversation. I felt close to her, not like other first date, you know."

The next day, I got a call from the girl's father. He asked all sorts of roundabout questions, then he finally came out with it. "Is there something wrong with this Yasha?" he asked.

Trouble.

"What do you mean?" I asked cautiously.

"Well, do you know what he chose to speak about on a first date?" he said, and then he went on to tell me all about the conversation. "My daughter couldn't believe it!"

"There is absolutely nothing wrong with Yasha," I reassured him. "You have to understand where he is coming from. Because he is from Russia, most of the girls he sees are totally not attuned to his way of thinking. Your daughter, however, was really attuned to him, and he felt so unbelievably comfortable with her. He understands perfectly well that such things are usually not discussed until the fourth date, but she was so suited to him that he felt there was an instant closeness. At least, in his mind."

The girl's father mulled over this explanation for a minute or two.

"All right," he said. "I think I understand what he was thinking. I just want everything to go calmly, with no one jumping to impulsive decisions."

"Of course," I said. "You needn't worry."

Disaster averted. So Yasha will continue to see the girl. Who knows how this will end? Perhaps with a *mazel tov*. Wouldn't that be nice?

So what I am trying to bring out with this story?

I think there is an important lesson to be learned here for husbands and wives. Sometimes misunderstandings can arise in a marriage, where one spouse may do or say something that the other thinks is inappropriate.

But stop and think for a moment. Isn't it possible that your husband may have done or said what he did because he feels so very close to you, just as Yasha did on his first date?

Instead of being upset, wouldn't it be better to take advantage of the opportunity to build on that closeness?

~

Dear Daughter,

Misunderstandings. Such a benign-sounding word. Yet such a dangerous one as well. Many a marriage has faltered on simple misunderstandings.

Misunderstandings, my dear child, are an inevitable part of life. It is almost impossible to have any sort of meaningful human relationship without occasional misunderstandings. They are like viruses carried by the breeze. If you breathe you can catch them.

But you don't have to die from a virus. Usually, with a little rest and extra care, a virus will run its course and disappear after a few days. Unless it is neglected. Then the virus can drag on and on, and eventually, it can even lead to very serious, life-threatening illnesses such as pneumonia.

The same applies to misunderstandings. Treat them right away with a little common sense and wisdom, and they will vanish without a trace. But let them linger and fester, and before you know it, you can have a very serious, full-blown problem in your marriage.

The first thing you must realize about misunderstandings between you and your husband is that they are the direct result of the special closeness that exists between you.

Think of the two of you as Siamese twins.

Two ordinary siblings may go about their respective business without ever seriously infringing upon each other. Very often, they are like ships passing in the night. Naturally, then, they can have a very fine relationship without constant little eruptions between them.

But this is not the case with Siamese twins. Every single move, every twitch that one sibling makes instantly creates a tug and a pull on the other. Quite often, that tug is painful, and it will elicit a shriek. But that is to be expected of two people so inextricably attached to each other. Eventually, these little tug and shrieks will lead to an even greater closeness as the two Siamese twins develop a profound sensitivity to each other and a rhythm which accommodates both of them perfectly.

This is what husband and wife are like. They are so close to each other, their lives are so closely intertwined with each other, that every little pull by one spouse elicits an immediate reaction from the other.

This is what Adam meant when he said of Chavah, "Bone of my bones." Unlike the lion and the lioness who are each worlds unto themselves with but the most fleeting and casual attachment to each other, husband and wife are part of one unit, one entity. That connectedness defines their entire relationship.

You know, you once asked me an interesting question relating to this subject. When you shared a room with other girls in summer camp, there were rarely any conflicts, and when they did occur, they were so easily resolved. On the other hand, minor conflicts are so much more likely to arise between you and your husband, and they are more difficult to resolve. And yet you both love each other and care about each other very deeply. Why is this so? Why should there be more difficulties between people who love each other than between casual friends?

A very good question. As for the answer, you actually touched upon it yourself in your question. It is precisely because you love each other that all these minor difficulties arise.

Your friends in camp are not that important to you. They are not part of the very essence of your life. So most of what they do just passes you by unnoticed. Why should it annoy you when it has very little to do with you? And if something does happen that upsets you, it certainly won't upset you very deeply. After all, it's all external to you anyway. So it's not too difficult to resolve the problem, forget about it and go on with your life.

With your husband, however, it's an altogether different story. You and he are so closely connected to each other that every little move either of you makes tugs and pulls at the other. It's no wonder then that you have so many more minor eruptions. And when they do happen, they're not so easy to brush aside. If your husband did not give you a sunny smile that day it is much more disturbing than if some friend hadn't smiled at you. And if it's more disturbing, it's harder to resolve.

But look at it this way. All these little misunderstandings and eruptions are just signs of how close you are, of how much you mean to each other. When your baby wakes in the night crying, it's not the easiest thing to get up and take care of him. But when it happens, you don't think of it as an annoyance. You go to him with love and joy. This is your baby! Only your own baby disturbs your sleep, not someone else's baby. Well, the same applies to your husband. When something disturbing occurs, deal with it with love. This is your husband and soul mate! It is only because he is so close to you that you are annoyed.

Use these little incidents as stimuli to bring the two of you even closer together. Work on developing such a rhythm and affinity to each other that even these little misunderstandings will eventually disappear.

Dear Daughter,

Speaking of misunderstandings, I would like to talk to you about one of the most common sources of trouble. It goes like this. Something has really upset you. You are walking around in a funk, thoroughly distressed. You heart is a flutter, and your mind is in a whirl. Your husband comes home and goes about his business as if nothing happened. He does not sense that your whole world is in turmoil, and you are infuriated by his lack of sensitivity. Sounds familiar?

Well, let me tell you another one of my stories.

There was a very great *rosh yeshivah* in Israel who used to come to the States every few months to raise money for his yeshivah as well as for many other worthy causes. Over the course of many years, he developed a very close personal relationship with a certain rich man. The *rosh yeshivah* and the rich man did not see each other that often, being so far apart. In those days, people hardly ever spoke to Israel on the telephone. Nonetheless, whenever they did get together their closeness was instantly revived. And so their friendship grew and flourished for years.

A few weeks after one of these periodic visits, the rich man's wife suddenly passed away. No one called the *rosh yeshivah* or told him about it, and so, being far away in Israel, he had no idea that tragedy had struck his American friend.

Six months later, the *rosh yeshivah* returned to the States. He went to visit the rich man and greeted him with his usual warmth.

"Now you show me all this warmth and friendliness?" said the rich man. "Where were you when I needed you? Why didn't you call me or at least send me a note when my wife passed away?"

The *rosh yeshivah* was shocked, of course, but he reacted in a very gentle manner. After a while, the rich man calmed down, and they spoke to each other until the wee hours of the morning.

Now, let's just think a moment about the rich man's first words to the *rosh yeshivah*. How unreasonable! How unfair! Surely, the rich man knew that the *rosh yeshivah* lived very far away and was extremely busy every minute of the day. How could he expect him to know about something that happened so far away, something that was known only in the immediate community? Why did he think the *rosh yeshivah* had no feelings for him?

The answer to this question is very revealing of human nature. The rich man's reaction was the result of the enormous pain and sorrow in his heart. His entire world had come crashing down with the death of his wife. In his own mind, the catastrophe was so thunderous that, irrationally, he thought that the *rosh yeshivah* must have heard it as well had he really cared about him.

He was wrong, of course. No matter how close two people are, no matter how deeply they care about each other, every human being is a world apart. And unless clear signals are sent, it is impossible to know what goes on in someone else's mind or heart.

My dear child, despite the great love you and your husband feel for each other, despite the common outlook on the world you share, the two of you are separate worlds. There will undoubtedly be times when some internal turmoil will thunder and rattle your world, but your husband will not always be aware of it. Just because you hear the roar, do not be so sure that he does. And if he does not respond to your distress, it does not mean that he is insensitive to you. He may simply be unaware of the extent of what you are feeling.

In such cases, you can cause great damage if you lash out at him in reaction to his supposed insensitivity.

Do not demand more from your husband than he is capable of doing. He can not always know what goes on inside your head. If you need his sympathy, speak to him about what you are feeling. Then he will surely give you all the sympathy and support that you need, because there is no one else in the world who is closer to you or cares more about you.

Believe me.

Dear Daughter,

I want to conclude this topic with a short letter about peace of mind. After all, the best way to avoid misunderstandings arising from inner turmoil is to eliminate inner turmoil as much as possible. How can this be done?

I recently read a first-person account of a woman whose husband became an alcoholic. It was a terrible tragedy. He ceased to function as a husband and father. His drunken bouts were frightening, and when he brought his drinking buddies home with him, it was even worse.

The woman loved her husband and understood that his actions were due to serious clinical depression. During the time of this ordeal, she struggled courageously to maintain a semblance of normalcy in her home for her young children while she sought treatment for her stricken husband.

In the end, her husband recovered, and the crisis thankfully passed.

While reading this story, I became aware of something very interesting. Despite all her troubles and travails, this woman seems to have been reasonably happy during this trying time in her life. She seems to have maintained a positive attitude and a sunny outlook.

Why didn't she fall apart under the weight of her terrible troubles? I think that many people would not have held up as well as she did.

And then the answer struck me. This woman was completely focused on preserving a happy, healthy atmosphere for her children, and when a person is focused, he has peace of mind. On an even deeper level, I realized how important a focus on the children is when it comes to preserving a happy home and a happy husband.

Along the same lines, Rav Yerucham Levovitz *zt"l*, the *Mashgiach* of the Mirrer Yeshivah, teaches us an important lesson on how to achieve permanent peace of mind. The key is focus. A person who is completely focused on serving Hashem, he explains, is guaranteed peace of mind. As long as the focus of his life is a powerful drive to serve Hashem, he will find that he can adjust to all conditions and all situations as he presses forward toward his ultimate goal.

We see this all the time. If someone undertakes a major project, such as building a new school, it absorbs all his thoughts, emotions and energy. Everything else becomes minor and secondary and really doesn't occupy a place in his mind. Anything, major or minor, that might have disturbed him under ordinary circumstances no longer plays a significant role and cannot disturb his peace of mind. Why? Because he is focused.

Anyone of us can do this, says Rav Yerucham. We don't have to build schools or struggle with tragedy in the household to become focused individuals. All we need to do is dedicate ourselves to serving Hashem.

Make that the focus of your life, and you will be guaranteed peace of mind.

— 13 —

Surgery in the Kitchen

Dear Daughter,

Do you know the best way to deliver criticism?

Let me tell you about a little boy who discovered the answer to this question. The boy's family had just moved into a new neighborhood, and they learned that the best school was Yiddish speaking. Although the parents knew Yiddish, the language was not spoken in their home. Nevertheless, they decided to send their young son to the Yiddish-speaking school.

At first, it was difficult for the boy, but young children adapt to new languages far more quickly than adults do. Within a few months, he was fairly fluent in Yiddish and doing very well in his studies.

One day, the boy said to his mother, "Mommy, my *rebbe* really loves me."

"I'm sure he does, sweetheart," she said. "What's not to love?"

"You know, my *rebbe* gives me blessings all the time."

"That's very nice."

"But there's something I don't understand," said the boy. "Why does he have to raise his voice and criticize me after he blesses me?"

The mother's ears perked up. "What do you mean?"

"Well, many times he tells me, '*Zie gezunt.*' That means be healthy. And then, after he blesses me, he criticizes me for different things I do."

The mother could hardly contain her laughter. In the Yiddish language, it is a figure of speech to preface criticism with a comment such as "*Zie gezunt*, may you be healthy," or "*Zalstu leben bis hundert un tzwantzig yahr*, may you live to be a hundred and twenty." The boy had taken this routine expression as a blessing.

The Yiddish language is holy, developed over many hundreds of years by Jews of high character and purity of soul, and there is a very good reason for this figure of speech. In fact, this is exactly how a Jew should deliver criticism, especially between husband and wife.

The Gemara tells us that "an angry woman destroys her home." Anger is such a terrible force that it can wreck the finest household. They weren't talking about a little flash of anger, which is inevitable from time to time, but an uncontrollable rage that can sweep away everything in its path.

You must never let your anger run out of control. It will only antagonize and alienate your husband, and nothing constructive will be accomplished. Better to take a hint from the Yiddish language. Begin with a few kind words before you give vent to your anger.

Remember that little boy and how he felt when his *rebbe* criticized him. His *rebbe* was blessing him! His *rebbe* loved him! Any criticism that followed such words could not wound him.

Tell that to your husband. Let him know you love him and

that there is no more important person in the whole world to you, and then you can tell him what has upset you. He will listen and do everything he can to make it right.

Someone once showed a letter he received from a famous *gadol*. It was sharply worded, full of rebuke and criticism. The letter began, "I love you but not your ideas and deeds." The letter made a deep impression upon him, and only because of those few introductory words. His whole attitude was affected by them, and he listened with an open mind.

The same holds true for a woman in her home. She doesn't have to be on the spiritual level of an angel to do this. It is all a matter of training and self-discipline. If she thinks into it and comes to the realization that "an angry woman destroys her home," as the Gemara states, she will find that this is the only way. Bless your husband before you castigate him.

So what about husbands? you ask.

Don't think I'm talking only to women. In *Sechel Tov*. I devoted many chapters to the importance of controlling anger. This is definitely a two-way street.

Dear Daughter,

There is a young man from Argentina who has been coming to visit me for 15 years. His name is Norberto Oro. His family name was originally Gold, but they changed it to Oro, the Spanish form of the word. I met him before his wedding when he came to ask about the Jewish outlook on marriage.

A year after his wedding, he came here on business, and he dropped in to see me. He was deliriously happy. But the next year and every year afterwards he grew more and more dejected.

What was the matter? It seems his wife regularly screamed at him and abused him verbally. No more how much he begged her to stop it, it was all to no avail.

One year, he told me he could bear no more. He had lost all feeling for his wife. Then he told me that his wife had come with him to America.

"Excellent," I said. "Perhaps we can get together and discuss your problems."

He shook his head. "No, we're going to get a divorce. There is no turning back."

"I see," I said. "Tell me, what does your wife have to say about this?"

"About the divorce? She doesn't know about it yet."

"Really? And how do you plan to break it to her?"

He shrugged. "I haven't decided yet."

"Well, why don't you bring her to me for a little talk? We can break it to her little by little. What do you say?"

Reluctantly, he agreed.

The next day, they came to my house. She seemed quite vivacious, completely oblivious to what was on her husband's mind.

"So, Mrs. Oro," I said after we were all settled, "I gather you came to discuss your *shalom bayis* problems."

Her eyes opened wide. "Rabbi! Whatever are you saying? We have no *shalom bayis* problems. We have the most beautiful *shalom bayis*."

What can I tell you? Both Norberto and I sat there with our mouths agape. We couldn't believe what we were hearing.

The silence dragged on and on. Finally, Norberto found his tongue.

"Perhaps we can discuss some specific situations," he suggested.

She seemed a little bewildered.

"I think this is a very good idea," I said. "You should both say everything that's on your minds, without reservations or inhibitions."

The discussion went on for several hours, and it was extremely helpful. Mrs. Oro wept bitterly when she realized how her marital situation had deteriorated without her knowing it. But then she listened attentively with a positive attitude. Thankfully, the marriage was saved.

Amazing, isn't? Her husband begs her for 13 years not to abuse him verbally, and she thinks they have beautiful *shalom bayis*!

Do you know what this means?

She didn't realize it.

You know that deaf people often speak very loudly. Why? Because they don't realize how loudly they are speaking. They do not hear well, so they speak loudly to hear themselves speak, without realizing how bizarre it sounds to other people. The same applies here. For some reason, she needed to express herself by using such sharp words, but she never realized how terrible they sounded to her husband. And even when he told her, she didn't really take him seriously.

My dear child, we all have to learn from this. If your husband ever comments on the way you express yourself, don't just brush it off. Take it seriously. Obviously, it means that something must be bothering him very much, and it may just be possible that your emotions are preventing you from realizing how painful your words are to him. Don't become defensive and try to justify yourself. That won't get you anywhere. It will just throw up more barriers between you.

Listen.

Hear.

And then discuss it calmly.

A peaceful discussion can avoid endless problems.

Dear Daughter,

I once heard a story about Rav Moshe Feinstein *zt"l* that made a strong impression on me, but I cannot vouch for its accuracy. I didn't hear it from someone who was present at the time nor did I read it in a reliable book. But whether or not it actually took place, it is a story with an important message, and the message is definitely true.

Rav Moshe once received a telephone call from a couple who were having serious *shalom bayis* problems. The conversation dragged on for a very long time, and Rav Moshe was becoming visibly fatigued. The *rebbetzin* begged him to hang up and go lie down, but Rav Moshe just shook his head and continued to listen and talk.

The *rebbetzin* came back again and again to ask him to cut the conversation short, but he would not comply. The *rebbetzin* was clearly becoming a little upset, but it did not help. Rav Moshe stayed on the telephone until both husband and wife had dealt with the problem to their satisfaction.

Afterwards, one of his *talmidim* decided to ask Rav Moshe a rather brazen question. "The *rosh yeshivah* must have seen how upset the *rebbetzin* was that he didn't hang up the telephone," the *talmid* said respectfully. "Does bringing *shalom bayis* to a stranger's home take precedence over *shalom bayis* in a person's own home?"

Rav Moshe smiled. "You are making a mistake. We don't have to make peace where there is no conflict. What is conflict? Two sides are angry and fighting each other. The man on the telephone was fighting with his wife, and she was fighting with him. That was a real *shalom bayis* problem. But in my case, my wife was not really very upset, and I wasn't upset at all. So there was no *shalom bayis* problem. Do you understand now why the telephone call took priority?"

This is such an important point to remember. In minor matters, there is no fight unless both sides participate.

Your husband, who is an exceptional *baal midos*, may sometimes make a remark that offends you. He may be under all kinds of pressure, which may cause him to react in a way that he shouldn't. I want you to know that you have a choice. If you lash back, there is a fight. But if you don't, then it is only an overflow of your husband's emotions, and it is about as serious as an over-flow of the kitchen sink. Neither is particularly pleasant, and both are no more than a temporary nuisance.

You can never go wrong by being strong and remaining silent. Let the storm pass before you react. You may later regret remarks which you shouldn't have made. You may want to take back certain things you said, which you can never do, of course. But you will never be sorry that you were silent, that you made no hurtful or sharp retorts.

I am reminded of a couple who were having terrible problems with a rebellious son. The situation had become so bad that they had thrown him out of the house, and he was living with distant relatives. We spent many hours discussing the situation, and it became clear that the only solution was to show their son how much they loved him.

After our discussions, the parents met with their son and expressed their love and their desire to have him come home. It worked. There was a reconciliation, and the boy was invited home. On the day of his return, the parents made a small party for him. I also attended. Everything was going beautifully when the conversation turned to a rather delicate subject, something which had been a sore point between parents and child. Suddenly, the teenager made an incredibly vicious remark about his parents.

I gasped, afraid that our carefully engineered reconciliation was about to explode. I looked at the parents anxiously, but I saw only smiles. Wisely, they had decided to let the remark pass with-out comment. At that moment, the fragile peace in their home could have fallen apart, but the love and wisdom of the parents saved it. At that moment, they understood the value of keeping silent, and they did. Today, their relationship with their wayward son is good, and it is getting better all the time.

My dear daughter, you have to understand the nature of young men. They are instinctively impatient and somewhat hot tempered. The Ramban writes that patience usually comes with age and experience. How very true! And so, no matter how much of a *baal midos* your husband may be, it is possible that he may sometimes be impulsive and do or say something that will annoy you.

Be strong. Remain silent.

Remember, if you do not react reflexively and retaliate, there is no fight.

The *Shelah* advises the woman to be conciliatory when her husband is angry. He does not mean that you should repress your feelings and ignore them. Rather, he wants you to set them aside and wait for the right moment when you can discuss them in a calm, level-headed manner.

Both you and your husband are full of love for each other, but you cannot expect love to flourish in an atmosphere charged with anger and resentment.

Be wise. Choose your moments.

Believe me, you will be doing both of yourselves a favor.

⌣——

Dear Daughter,

How would you like to hear about an interesting scenario I cooked up? I know you're going to object that certain elements of it are unrealistic, but it doesn't matter. It is just meant to bring out a point.

The scene is a winter afternoon in my living room. There is a blinding blizzard outside. The streets are knee-deep in snow and all but impassable. An icy wind is howling, but in my living room it is warm and cozy. I am sitting and drinking tea with my good friend, Dr. Schwartenbach. We grew up together in Buenos Aires, and we still keep in touch.

As we reminisce about old times, there is a loud, frantic knock at the door. I open the door. It is our neighbor, Mrs. Blumenthal.

"Help me! Help me!" she screams. "My husband has collapsed on the kitchen floor. I can't call for help, because my telephone is dead. The lines are probably down. And look outside! What am I supposed to do? How can I get him to a hospital or get an ambulance to come here? Oh, what will I do? I'm afraid my husband is dying."

"Don't panic, Mrs. Blumenthal," I reassure her. "Fortunately, there is a very famous doctor right here in my house. We will come with you."

Doctor Schwartenbach grabs his black bag and accompanies me to the Blumenthal house next door.

Mr. Blumenthal is lying on the floor, holding his stomach and writhing in agony. Doctor Schwartenbach crouches down to examine him.

"It's his appendix," he finally announces. "He must be operated on immediately. We can't waste a minute if we are to save his life."

"But how can we get him to the hospital?" I protested. "We are completely snowed in."

"I realize that," he replied. "We must operate right here. Right on the kitchen table. Boil up a lot of water, and get some clean sheets. Hurry!"

Don't ask me why Doctor Schwartenbach had anesthetics, a scalpel, hemostats and sutures in his little black bag. I'm the author of this story, and I put them there. And it's a good thing I did, because they saved Mr. Blumenthal's life. The combination of Doctor Schwartenbach's surgical skills and the equipment I provided brought off a small miracle, and we had a successful appendectomy right there on the Blumenthal's kitchen table.

Quite a hair-raising story, isn't it?

Something like this could only happen in a wild snowstorm or in someone's wild imagination, or a combination of both. Otherwise, why in the world would someone perform surgery in a kitchen? Right?

Wrong.

Unfortunately, surgery is performed in thousands of kitchens every single day when husbands and wives criticize each other without regard for each other's feelings. After all, don't sharp words of criticism cut like a knife? Of course they do. Criticism delivered with patience, kindness and love is a true blessing, but criticism delivered in anger is like a scalpel without anesthetic.

You can't just criticize your husband, or vice versa, in the middle of the whirl and swirl of a normal household. Even the most refined and unassuming husband will feel he has had surgery performed on him in the kitchen. Patients have a hard time recovering from surgery in the kitchen. And the "doctors" who perform their surgery in the kitchen suffer equally when their operations are unsuccessful.

No, you must find a time when you are both calm, when it is quiet in the house. Then you must begin with warm and compassionate words. They are like an anesthetic that will prevent the pain of what comes next. Only then can you bring up your criticism in a very positive and constructive way.

This is the way to perform delicate, painless surgery to nip a small problem in the bud before it can interfere with the wonderful harmony of your home.

— 14 —

Minor Annoyances

Dear Daughter,

Do you ever wonder why some couples have beautiful marriages and others don't? Even when all things seem equal, the same kind of people, the same backgrounds, the same living conditions, we still find that some couples are successful and others are not. Why?

An interesting parable in *Sefer Madreigas Haadam* sheds some light on this question.

There was once a king who built a palace with very tall walls. He placed a long ladder against one of the walls and issued a challenge to his subjects. The first one to scale the wall by climbing the ladder to the very top would be rewarded with the royal princess's hand in marriage and a treasure house full of riches.

There was a trick, however. One of the steps of the ladder, which appeared to be exactly identical to all the others, was actually rigged to make the climber lose his balance.

Many hopeful subjects attempted to scale the wall, but each one of them lost his balance and fell back to the ground. Finally, the crowd assembled at the foot of the wall began to grumble.

"This is all just to tease us," people were saying. "It is impossible to scale that wall."

One clever fellow, however, refused to believe it. He knew the king to be a wise and kind man, not at all the type who would play spiteful tricks on his subjects. Surely, this was a very real test to find the one clever enough to find the solution. Only he would be worthy of the king's daughter.

And so, this clever fellow sat back and watched the others carefully. After a while, he noticed that each one of them was losing his balance on one particular step.

When his turn to came, he clambered up the ladder until he reached that step. Then he gingerly skipped over it and continued on to the top of the wall.

A little thought had won him incredible good fortune.

It is the same in marriage. All marriages have a trick step concealed somewhere. The clever people have sought out and found that step, and they know how to avoid it. Their marriages are usually happy and successful. The others keep blundering onto that step and fall to the ground.

So what is that step? And how do we find it?

Ah, that is what the entire world would like to know.

On one of my trips to visit my parents in Argentina, I had a brief stopover in Sao Paolo, Brazil. As I strolled through the busy streets, I noticed that many people were streaming into an enormous building, as big as the Javits Center in New York. There must have been literally thousands of them.

What could this be? A championship ball game?

My curiosity got the better of me, and I went to investigate. It turned out to be far more interesting than a mere ball game. It seems that a certain Dr. Castro was giving a lecture about his secret formula for a happy marriage. I didn't have time to investigate any further, because I had to get back to my plane. It did give me much food for thought.

Happy marriages! How desperately people wanted to have happy marriages. They would even line up by the thousands to listen to Dr. Castro, whoever he was, just for the chance of improving their married lives. I wondered if many of these people came away from this lecture with anything substantial, besides empty words and hot air. I tend to doubt it. Except for Dr. Castro, of course, who undoubtedly came away with a substantial amount of money.

I do know one thing. Our Sages had the formula, and they revealed it to us. King Solomon, the wisest man who ever lived, writes, "And you are to know that there will be peace in you rdwellings."

What does he mean? Our Sages explain that peace will dwell in our homes if we sharpen our knives on Erev Shabbos. Furthermore, the *Mishnah Berurah* states in the Laws of Shabbos: "Sharpen your knives on Erev Shabbos, so that you will have peace in your home."

That's right. If we sharpen our knives on Erev Shabbos.

You are perplexed? I don't blame you.

Is this some kind of a magical thing? Is it a *segulah* that works in the mystical spheres?

I don't think so. I think it has a very clear, down-to-earth explanation.

Let us conjure up two Friday night scenes in our imagination. We will be visiting two couples and eavesdropping on their conversations. But don't worry, they won't see us. And you needn't worry about the propriety of what we will be doing, because these people don't really exist.

So! Are you ready for takeoff?

Here we are at the Cohens. It's right before Shabbos.

"You know, Pesach is just around the corner," says the lady of the house. "We need to make some plans. I think we should go to my parents for Pesach. After all, we spent last Pesach with your parents."

"You're right," says her husband as he busily sharpens the *challah* knife. "We did spend last Pesach with my parents, but I think we should go there again this year. You know what your parents' house is like on Pesach with all the company they have. I really find it hard and uncomfortable. On the other hand, my parents really don't have anyone else. I think they could use our company much more, and we would be so comfortable. It would be such a pleasant *yom tov*."

"I hear what you're saying, but comfort isn't everything. It is very important to me to be at my father's *Seder* table at least once in a while. I think that — whoops! Look what time it is. I have to go light the candles. We can talk about this later."

She goes off to light the candles. He goes off to *shul*.

Later on that evening, they sit down to the *seudah*. He makes the *berachah* over the fragrant *challos*. Then he takes the *challah* knife and begins to slice. The knife is so sharp that it cuts through the *challah* like butter and leaves beautiful whole pieces. They both eat the delicious *challah* and settle down to the meal.

During the meal, the subject of Pesach comes up again. They discuss it in a calm and cooperative manner, and they reach a solution that is satisfactory to both of them.

Wonderful.

Now let us visit the Schwartzes. Again, it is right before Shabbos.

"We have to decide about Pesach," says the lady of the house. "You know that it's my parents' turn to have us this year, don't you?"

"I won't argue with you about that," says her husband as the *challah* knife lies undisturbed on the table. "But it's a problem. I can never relax in your parents' house. Our room is so small and cramped, and there is so much noise. I usually come home exhausted. Couldn't we go to my parents this year? It's so quiet and restful in their house, and they really miss us."

"I miss them, too, but how do you think my parents will feel about it? It means a lot to them to have us come for Pesach. They may have a full house, but we are really important — whoops! Candle lighting time. Let's continue this later."

She goes off to light the candles. He goes off to *shul*. Amazing how similar these situations are, isn't it?

Presently, the husband returns. He makes *Kiddush*, and they sit down to the *seudah*. He make the *berachah* over the fragrant *challos*. Then he takes the *challah* knife and begins to slice. But the knife is dull, and instead of slicing through the *challah*, it just leaves a long depression across the top without breaking the surface.

He pushes harder, sawing mightily at the soft *challah*, but it doesn't do much good. The strain is showing on his face as he pushes down with all his might. The knife finally breaks through the *challah*, but it rips rather than cuts, leaving long ragged strands. He manages to separate a half-shredded piece for himself and another for his wife. There is no smile on his face as he hands her the piece of *challah*.

During the meal, the subject of Pesach comes up again.

"You know, you never think about what will make me happy," he snaps. "Why should my Pesach be ruined by going to your parents?"

The hurt springs to her eyes, which quickly fill up with tears. "Is that so?" she snaps back. "You —"

I think it's time we slipped away from the Schwartz house, don't you? It's obvious that a very ugly scene is brewing, and I don't think we should stay around to watch.

So, my dear daughter, how do we explain the difference between the Cohen and the Schwartzes? Both are strong-minded people, and the dilemmas they face are very similar. And yet, the Cohens reach an amiable resolution, while the Schwartzes go to war.

What is the difference?

It is the sharpened knife. The knife in the Cohen home was sharp, and when the husband cut the *challah*, everything went smoothly. When the discussion about their Pesach plans continued, he was in a pleasant state of mind, and they were able to work it out in a mature way.

But the knife in the Schwartz home was dull. When the husband cut the *challah*, he became very nervous and frustrated, and when his wife brought up the subject of Pesach, he lashed out at her.

A small thing like a dull knife, yet look at all the trouble it can cause. That is the way it is with human nature. Little things can disrupt a person's peace of mind, and then he can react in totally inappropriate ways when he is confronted by a difficult situation.

This is what our Sages, in their infinite wisdom, were telling us. "Sharpen your knife!" Make sure you avoid all the minor, easily corrected annoyances that can disrupt the peace and harmony of your household. Especially, when there are differences of opinion between you – and there always will be – don't discuss them when you are tense and upset. With good sense, mutual tolerance, and calm, you can almost always work things out, but it is much, much harder if you are under stress or pressure.

Let me just mention one of these minor annoyances which surely comes up all the time.

The Shelah advises the wife to pay particular attention to mealtimes. "She should make sure that the food is ready at mealtimes. If her husband is a *talmid chacham*, he should not have to lose learning time. If he is a businessman, he should not have to lose earning time."

Many men, probably most, don't get upset if a hot plate of soup is not waiting on the table when they come home. But if your husband is one of those who is so particular about his mealtime, then don't let such a trivial thing get in the way of your happy marriage.

It's not a very major task to have the food ready on time, is it? Yet a minor annoyance such as this can disrupt your husband's peace of mind and cause you unnecessary problems.

$\backsim$

Dear Daughter,

Even before I got your last letter, I knew exactly what it would say. Sharpening the knives for Shabbos would be no problem, but having the food ready on time? That was an entirely different story. After all, you are only a human being, not an automaton. Being married is not like being in the army, where everything must run like clockwork.

My child, you are right, but every human being has the right to some personal quirks. The same applies to you. There may be one or two things about you that annoy him, but he should be intelligent enough to overlook them or try to cater to your needs. Is it really so difficult to have your husband's food ready on time? In the same letter, you write that your baby woke up at 3 in the morning, and you had to spend a half-hour with him. So tell me, where did you get the strength to tear yourself out of bed at 3 o'clock in the morning?

The answer is simple. You are a mother, and you naturally respond to the needs of your child, even though you would rather turn over on the other side and go back to sleep.

Think for a moment if you husband needs you to be punctual. It may be very important to him, although you might not relate to it personally.

For instance, a businessman may feel that if he is late to work he will lose an important account. A *kollel* member might feel that if he is late his *chavrusa* will be upset, and it will be more difficult for him to find a good *chavrusa* in the future. Whether or not he is right, the anxiety he may be feeling is very real, and it can easily destroy his good mood and general good spirits. Once that happens, it is downhill all the way.

Keep in mind, my dear daughter, that although I am speaking to you, the same advice applies to your husband, as I wrote to the men in *Sechel Tov*.

So tell me, have you ever seen a car explode in a gas station? No? Well, neither have I. Nor have I ever seen people smoking while they are filling their gas tanks. People are smart enough to take simple precautions to avoid danger.

The same applies to your husband. If you just take a few simple precautions, you can avoid putting your *shalom bayis* at risk. If having his meals on time affects his mood, then it is important that you do so. It may require a little extra effort on your part, but it can be done. I have never heard of a Jewish homemaker who was not ready for the *Seder* on Pesach night. If it must be done, it will be done.

Judge for yourself what must be done in your own household, and what does not need to be done. If it helps your husband avoid unnecessary tension and anxiety, it is well worth the effort.

— *15* —

Keeping the Peace

Dear Daughter,

Do you remember when we went to your little brother's Chanukah performance? The children were so cute in their colorful costumes. And do you remember their choir? You thought it was the funniest thing. Every child was singing at a different pitch on a different key. What a cacophony! It wasn't a concert, just a tremendous clutter of sounds. We all laughed and thought it was very adorable, but it wasn't exactly pleasing music.

On the other hand, a really good choir is just wonderful to hear, especially when the singers are harmonizing together. Here again we have singers on different keys, but when it's well coordinated, the effect is great.

What determines when we have cacophony and when we have harmony? Well, for one thing it naturally has a lot to do with the quality and talent of the singers, wouldn't you agree?

But there is also another important factor.

Once when I was in a car with an old friend, classical music was playing on the radio as we talked. Suddenly, he stopped talking, bent over the radio and turned up the volume. A majestic new piece was starting.

"That's Beethoven's Eroica Symphony," he whispered reverentially. "Isn't it just magnificent?"

"Sure, sure," I said. It actually did sound pretty good. Obviously it was familiar to him.

I saw he was listening intently, as if he was strain to hear something. I wondered what it was.

"Yep, I'm sure of it," he finally said. "That's Leonard Bernstein conducting."

"What!" I reacted in astonishment. "Do you mean to tell me you can tell who the conductor is?"

"It's not that hard," he said. "Every conductor has his own style. It's quite distinctive, you know."

I didn't know, but I guess I knew now. It was quite a revelation for me.

So where is all of this leading? To life, of course.

My dear child, I wrote to you earlier about the opposite natures of men and women. Men and women are on different wavelengths, different pitches, different keys. When those different notes are blended together beautifully, we have the sweet sounds of harmony. Peace reigns in the home. But when those different notes are in discord, when they raise a cacophony instead of harmony, it is jarring to the ears and to the heart. Peace is lacking from the home.

So who decides if we will have cacophony or harmony? It is the conductor whose talents and skill blend the different cadences into one beautiful sound. And who is the conductor? That's right. You guessed it. You are the conductor.

"Chochmas nashim bansah beisah," King Solomon tells us. "Woman's wisdom built her home."

What is this special wisdom of the woman? According to the Vilna Gaon, women have the ability to think responsibly without being impulsive. They will not sacrifice long-term gains for the gratification of the moment. When Rachel discovered that her father Lavan had fooled her, she could easily have sent a message to Yaakov to apprise him of the situation. But she didn't. The Midrash tells us that she understood that by doing so she could lose any chance she had of ever marrying Yaakov. This wisdom guided her actions and ensured that eventually she married Yaakov and became one of the matriarchs of the Jewish people. This is the type of wisdom that is critical for the establishment of peace in the home. The Shelah also writes that it is in the power of the woman to create great peace between husband and wife.

By the way, don't think for a moment that I am placing the entire responsibility for peace in the home on the shoulders of the wife. I wrote very strong words to the men in *Sechel Tov*. In any case, it is the woman who is the conductor of the home. The conductor's baton is in her hands. She is the one who can blend all the sounds and experiences in the home into one beautiful harmony and bring lasting peace into the home.

The first thing a conductor must know is that he is working with different instruments, each of which has its own distinct sound. He must know what to expect from each of them, and what not to expect. The same applies to a marriage. Let me tell you a little story.

A young recently married woman once complained to me about her husband. He was always kind to her but very reserved. She accepted it as just the way he is, and she was content. One day, a friend of his came over to the house. They sat down to talk in the living room, while she took care of a few things in the kitchen. Suddenly, she heard a loud burst of laughter from the other room. She looked in and saw her husband in a totally new mode. He was talkative and exuberant, laughing uproariously. She found this very disturbing. She had never really seen this bubbly side to his personality, and she was offended he didn't show it when he was with her.

"There is no need to be offended," I told her. "You just have to understand the difference between men and women. A distant relative of mine is a teacher in an inner city school. You know what some of those places can be like, don't you? Guns, knives, drugs, who knows what else."

"I can imagine," she said.

"And yet, my relative is a successful teacher. I asked him how he does it. How does he keep control of this class? You know what he told me? It's all in the seating arrangement. He never sits a boy next to a boy or a girl next to a girl. Whatever else goes on between these boys and girls, they are not very likely to get absorbed in lengthy conversations with each other and disrupt the class. They simply have fundamentally different interests and do not very often 'bubble' with each other for hours. It works. There is usually very little talking among the students in his classroom. Do you understand how this applies to you?"

"Tell me," said the young woman.

"If your husband is not as animated with you as he is with some of his friends, it does not mean that he loves you any less. It simply means that males are on the same wavelength, and they respond to each other in different ways. I'm sure your husband loves you very deeply."

The young woman went away very happy and content. She didn't really need her husband to 'bubble' with her. She just felt slighted that he had 'bubbled' with his friend and not with her. But there was no reason to be offended. What had happened was only natural.

As the conductor in your household, my dear daughter, you must recognize which sounds are natural and which are not and blend everything together so that your home will be filled with sweet harmony and a beautiful sense of peace.

Another important thing you must keep in mind as the conductor, the maestro of your home, is a sense of timing. Let us say, for example, that something happens between you and your husband on Friday afternoon. Maybe your husband says something to which you take exception. Or maybe your say something to which he takes exception. Do you deal with it right away or leave it for a while?

The wisdom of a clear-thinking woman would let it ride for a little while. Friday afternoon is a high-tension time in a Jewish household. The wife is stressed and hassled, there are so many things to do. The husband is tired from a long week, overloaded with last-minute errands and usually running late. This is obviously not the time to raise issues. Better to wait for Shabbos to bring its blessings into the home, to lower the level of stress and anxiety and raise the level of *kedushah* and gentle love.

You, my dear child, are the conductor. The baton is in your hand. It is up to you to bring the sweet sounds of harmony into your home with your wisdom, your sensitivity, your exquisite sense of timing. It is up to you to make it a haven of peace.

— 16 —

Winners Are Losers

Dear Daughter,

Now that you are a married lady with a home and children of your own, those summers you spent in camp when you were a young girl must seem very far away. Well, let me remind you of a certain visiting day which still stands out in my mind, and I am sure in yours as well.

It was a drizzly, miserable day, and the drive up to camp in the mountains took us well over three hours. But we never even considered not going. Visiting day is so important to campers, and we were so eager to see your shining face.

Unfortunately, your face was shining in a different way that day. It glistened with tears.

"What happened?" your mother and I cried out at the same time.

"Color war," you said and burst into tears all over again.

Your mother and I looked at each other, puzzled.

"I don't understand," I said. "Is winning color war so important that you have to cry if you lose?"

You looked at me with horror in your eyes and began to cry even harder.

"What's going on?" I said. "So you lost color war. So what?"

You shook your head. "I didn't lose," you said. "I won. And that's the trouble." And then a new torrent of tears came flowing down. I threw up my hands in despair. Adolescent daughters!

Well, finally you calmed down and were able to talk a little.

"I won color war," you said, "but I lost my best friend."

"I see," I said, although I didn't see a thing. But it was something to say.

"Me and my friend Miriam," you continued, "they put us on opposite sides for color war. We wanted to be on the same team, but they didn't listen to us. So we were on opposite teams. Anyway, we both got so involved with winning. We both wanted to win so badly that we thought about nothing else. For those two days, we wanted nothing more than to beat each other. And then when color war was over, things just weren't the same. So you see why I'm upset? I won color war but I lost my best friend!"

I'm sure you remember this day. It's not something a person ever forgets.

Unfortunately, what happened to you and Miriam in camp happens all too often in everyday relations between people, and it can really destroy a relationship.

The drive to be victorious is part of the darker side of human nature. It is more than just the desire to excel and be successful in anything you try, which is a very good thing that can have positive results in every aspect of your life. This, however, is something else. It is the need to be victorious over another person. If there is a struggle, we have to win; no matter how small the reward, no matter what the cost. Winning is the thing.

That was what happened to you in camp that summer. Both you and Miriam were overcome by this primal need to win, and it destroyed your friendship. Temporarily, of course. You both came to your senses eventually and made up, and your friendship thrives even today. I am very happy about that. But you know, of course, that your friendship could just as easily have died right there in the middle of color war in summer camp. It has happened to too many people.

This terrible thing called the urge to win is one of the most destructive forces in a marriage. It can literally kill it. In a marriage there are always all sorts of disagreements and different points of view. You want to eat fish. He wants to eat meat. You want a minivan. He wants a car. You want to go to Israel. He wants to go to California. You want to go to your parents for Shabbos. He wants to stay home. And so on. Hundreds of things, some major, some minor, all of them points of contention.

The most frightening thing is that it can strike before you even know it. Suddenly, you are in a contest of wills with your husband, a real tug of war. You want one thing, and he wants another. You are arguing heatedly about it. But if you stop to think about, you will wonder, what is so important here? Why are you both getting so excited about this issue? Is it really so important? More often than not, you know what it is? You both want to win. Your desire to win is crashing up against his desire to win. The main thing now is to win, not the issue itself.

If this happens, you are headed down a dangerous road. It doesn't lead to good places. Because even if you win, you lose. You may win the argument. You may be victorious in the contest of wills and get your way, but the damage to your relationship with your husband is an incredibly high price to pay for a silly little victory. You have to be aware of this all the time, and if or when you see it happening, you have to step back to regain perspective.

I remember speaking to a couple who were experiencing marital problems and were seriously contemplating divorce.

"My husband is totally impossible," the wife told me. "We just do not see eye to eye."

"Really?" I said. "Can you give me the most recent example?"

"Sure," she said. She thought for a moment. "This morning we went to the grocery to buy coffee. I wanted to buy Folgers, and he just insisted that we buy Maxwell House. He absolutely would not give in."

"I see," I said. This time I actually did see. These people were a long way down the wrong road. They were invested in winning against each other, no matter the cost. It took a lot of work, but I am pleased to say, we were able to save the marriage. In fact, when they opened their eyes to what was going on, they were shocked that they had been prepared to dissolve their marriage for such a trivial reason.

Some time ago, I visited a friend's sick child, an 8-year-old boy who was laid up in the hospital for a long time. While I was there, the child's *rebbi* showed up.

The boy's face lit up when he saw his *rebbi*, and from the look on the *rebbi's* face, I could see that the love was reciprocal.

"Here, I brought you a gift," said the *rebbi* as he handed him a gift-wrapped oblong package.

The boy eagerly unwrapped the gift, but when he saw what it was, he was disappointed.

"It's a checkers set," he said, "but I don't know how to play."

"No problem," said the *rebbi*. "I'll teach you."

And so the *rebbi* taught the boy how to play checkers, and they began to play. At first, it was very obvious to all of us there, except maybe for the sick boy, that the *rebbi* was deliberately letting him win. He squealed with delight every time he got one of the *rebbi's* pieces, and when he won the game, he was ecstatic.

"Let's play again," he begged. And so they played a second, third, fourth and even fifth game. The *rebbi* let the boy win every single game, to his intense enjoyment.

As the games progressed, however, it became apparent that the boy had caught onto the game and was doing very well.

Several times, the *rebbi* had to struggle to get out of a situation into which the boy had forced him. In fact, it wouldn't have surprised us if the boy had won a game on his own.

Afterwards, I complimented the *rebbi* on his visit and the wonders it had done for the boy.

"It looked as if he gave you a really good fight in the checkers game," I added with a smile.

The *rebbi* gave me a peculiar look. "You know," he said, "today I learned an important lesson. In the beginning, when I had just taught him the game, I had an easy time with him. Of course, I let him win, because I wanted to make him happy. But as he began to get the hang of the game and play better and better, he became real competition. And then a strange thing happened. I found myself trying to win! I actually had to force myself to make poor moves and let the boy win."

I nodded with understanding. "The urge to win," I said.

"Exactly. I felt this compulsion to fight for victory. 'Fool,' I told myself. 'What do you think you're doing here? Competing for the checkers championships? You're here to help a sick child. Let him win!' So I listened to myself, and I let him win. But it was a scary experience, and it taught me an important lesson. The urge to win, as you call it, is a very dangerous thing."

Indeed it is.

Overcoming the urge to win is extremely difficult, because you are fighting against the *yetzer hara*. The urge to win comes from the same source as arrogance. The *yetzer hara* convinces a person that he must always be right and therefore he must always fight for absolute victory.

This is a bad *middah*, and we must work hard to break it, as with all bad *middos*. But it can be done with wisdom and patience.

A person who is quick to anger will wait on a customer patiently and politely because he doesn't want to lose business. His intelligence and self-interest enable him to overcome his natural tendency.

The same applies here. When you feel that compulsion to win, think of what the costs are. Just as that *rebbi* was able to control the urge by reminding himself that the whole purpose of being there was to make the sick child feel good, not to win at checkers. You, too, can use this approach to control the urge to win.

Should such a situation ever arise between you and your husband, think of what you have and what you are risking by going down this dangerous road. You have a wonderful husband, a beautiful home, your own little *Beis Hamikdash* in this world, a pure, holy and happy life. Why should you risk everything on a foolish, irrational urge to gain a meaningless victory?

Just remember to ask yourself that question. No answers are needed.

— 17 —

The Money Bug

Dear Daughter,

Money looms large in people's lives. It never ceases to amaze me to what extent people will go for their money.

Let me tell you an interesting story that I heard from my father.

As you know, my parents were originally from Germany. When the Nazis came to power, everything fell apart for them. After enduring anti-Semitic persecution for a few years, they had the good sense to leave behind their money and all their possessions and flee to Argentina. Not everyone was so fortunate.

My father once told me about a friend of his who was fabulously wealthy. He knew he had to leave the country, but it was against the law to take any valuables along. Anyone who got caught trying to smuggle valuables out of Germany was sent off to a concentration camp. My father's friend didn't know what to do.

One day, he had a brilliant idea. He converted all his possessions to gold. Then he had a solid-gold automobile bumper made out of all his bullion. He covered the bumper with a layer of ordinary metal, then he attached it to his car. No one looking at the car could possibly know that its bumper was worth millions. All he had to do was drive the car across the border and he would be a free and rich man. The brilliance of the idea lay in its very simplicity.

As he approached the checkpoint at the border, he saw there was a long line of cars waiting to cross before him. He took his place in the line and waited.

As you can well imagine, the wait took a terrible toll on his nerves.

Finally, it was his turn. The border guard waved him forward. he eased the car into gear, but in his anxiety, he stepped too heavily on the accelerator. The car surged forward and slammed into the car ahead of him. The veneer on the bumper broke, and the gold underneath was revealed.

My father's friend was instantly arrested. He was sent to the Dachau concentration camp and never heard from again.

So what do you think of this man? Do you think he is admirable?

Many people I speak to think he did the right thing. They respect him for figuring out a way to outsmart the Nazis. He had a brilliant idea, and it was just his misfortune that he crashed the car at the last moment.

According to the view of our Sages, however, what this man did was not at all praiseworthy. He is considered a person who loves his money more than his life.

Why? Because no matter how brilliant his idea may have been, there is always an element of risk. Something can always go wrong, as indeed it did.

This man could have abandoned all his possessions and left

Germany, just as my parents did. But he chose instead to execute a brilliant but risky plan to outsmart the Nazis so that he could have his freedom and his money. In essence, therefore, he risked his life for his money. The Torah does not approve of that. Nothing is more precious than the gift of life, and it must not be risked for anything.

So I just told you another one of my stories. What does this have to do with a Jewish marriage? A lot.

Just as you understand that it is ridiculous to risk your precious life for the sake of money, so too is it ridiculous to risk your precious marriage for the sake of money.

You know, one of the more serious sins in the Torah is to erase the Name of Hashem. And yet, the Torah tells us that if a man suspects his wife of being unfaithful, the holy Name of Hashem is dissolved in water which she is then given to drink. If nothing happens, she is proved innocent.

Do you see how precious a marriage is to the Almighty? In order to preserve the relationship between husband and wife, Hashem allows His holy Name to be erased!

So tell me, should something so precious be put at risk for the sake of money?

I think not.

Dear Daughter,

You are so young and idealistic that it is a little difficult to write to you about these things. Money is important, but if you lose perspective, it can become a very terrible thing.

Young people have a dual problem with money. On the one hand, they see money as a life-and-death issue, blowing its importance out of all proportion. On the other hand, they think that their marital bliss and their loving relationship with their spouses will not be affected by the money problems. They are wrong on both counts.

As you grow older, you will discover that your health, your values, your family, your relationships and your sense of personal fulfillment are the things that count in life. Money is only a material thing, and your life does not depend on it. My father's friend would have been far better off without that gold bumper on his car. He might have been sitting today in Argentina or New York or Israel with young grandchildren on his lap. Now that is something precious and important. I'm not saying, of course, that money is not an important issue in marriage. It is an issue that comes up almost daily between husband and wife, and if you don't want it to spoil your marriage, you have to be very careful.

Once you let money become an issue, it gets into everything and contaminates it. Even if you don't see it, the money bug, as I call it, is there. It is like a piece of Romaine lettuce. You look at it and it seems to be clean as a whistle. But hold it up to the light, and there you will see those little bugs crawling all over the place. The money bug is the same thing. If you let it loose, it could crawl into all the little corners of your life and affect in ways you would not even recognize. I've learned this from experience, and believe me, this knowledge has saved me a lot of time and trouble.

A young fellow once came to me to discuss a girl he was seeing. We spoke for hours about his questions and reservations regarding the girl's personality, without reaching any conclusive results. I was a little puzzled. Then he dropped a small comment about a financial issue, and suddenly, I understood the whole thing. He may not have realized it himself, but he wasn't really concerned about her personality. It was the money bug that was prodding him!

From then on, I learned my lesson. If there are problems, look for the money! Now, one of the first things I ask about is the money issue, which very often takes me immediately to the heart of the problem. Isn't there a saying that "money is the root of all evil"? There's something to that. Dig deep enough, and there's a good chance you will find the money bug.

If you remember, I once took you to a great doctor when you

were a teenager. He was so kind and gentle, and such a skilled specialist; we both marveled at what an angel he was. Well, let me tell you about another side of him that I saw at the time but you didn't. When I went into his office to discuss his bill, this kind healer turned into a money-hungry brute. The money bug! Walk out of the examination room and into the billing office, and there it is!

Just look at the story of Yaakov and Lavan. When Yaakov first came, Lavan was very excited. He had heard that Yaakov was an intelligent, trustworthy, righteous man, a miracle worker no less! What better man to put in charge of his entire domain? Here was the perfect candidate for an important leadership position.

And then the money bug showed itself. Lavan remembered Eliezer's visit many years before, and he knew that Yaakov came from a fabulously wealthy family. Lavan fully expected Yaakov to be very wealthy in his own right. But then he discovered that Yaakov was penniless, and he had a complete turnaround. According to the Midrash, he told Yaakov, "What are you worth, penniless man? No more than a meatless bone!"

What had happened to all Yaakov's personal qualities? What had happened to all his skills and talents? Suddenly, they were all forgotten, swept away by the money bug. The same thing can happen, Heaven forbid, in a marriage. If money issues are given prominence, the whole relationship can be turned on its ear. A wife who had only admiration for her husband's sterling qualities will suddenly see only his faults, shortcomings and weaknesses.

So how do you deal with the money bug in your marriage? You keep it locked in a little room, and you only visit it at certain specified times. After your visit you leave and lock the door behind you. And make sure the money bug remains in the room and doesn't slip out together with you.

Am I being mysterious? Not really. What I'm saying is really very simple. Make up with your husband that you will only discuss money issues at certain specified times and never, never at any other time. This way you will deal with the issues quickly and cleanly and not have the money bug follow you around all day wherever you go.

Take an example from that doctor we visited. He never shows his money-hungry side in the examination room, because that would ruin his practice. No, he is smarter than that. He is all smiles and graciousness in the examination room, but for the few minutes he spends in the business office, he is all business and greed.

Can you imagine the caterer or photographer at a wedding bringing up his bill with the father of the bride during the first dance? Inconceivable, you say? Of course. These people know when to discuss money and when not to discuss it.

You must have the same guidelines in your marriage. When you are savoring all the wonderful experiences of marriage, don't spoil it by raising money issues. Keep the money bug away. Lock him away in a little room, and go visit him with your husband for a short while when you absolutely have to. If you do so, your married life will be full of joy.

I once saw a taxi driver dodging traffic as he ran after a passenger who short-changed him $3. The taxi driver was completely focused on his money, because he lives with the money bug all day. On the other hand, schools will rarely expel a child because of tuition problems. Do you know why? Because a school is not a business; at least it shouldn't be. Schools are focused on education, not money. They only charge tuition because they have to.

The same applies to your marriage. You marriage is not a business. It is a loving relationship, a partnership for life. You have to deal with the money bug, but money must never be a priority in your marriage.

I have a wealthy friend who is quite a miser but very happily married. I once paid him a visit on behalf of a certain very worthy charity. We spoke at length about the important work of this organization, but it didn't do me any good. He declined to make a contribution of any sort.

While all this was going on, his wife sat there silently. But a week later, I received a letter from her together with a substantial check. She explained that the check was drawn on funds that were completely at her discretion but still she did not want her husband to know about her donation. He might see it as a reprimand of his refusal to contribute, although it was nothing of the sort. She simply wanted to help out.

What a wonderful lady! She had the wisdom to prevent money from becoming a priority in her life. Although she had definite differences with her husband about money issues, she would not allow the money bug to interfere with their beautiful relationship.

You know that I always talk to my *talmidim* about the risks of driving and how irresponsible it is to risk one's life for the sake of thrills and adventure. Sometimes, I get the feeling that it goes in one ear and out the other. But one day, there was a terrible car accident right in front of the yeshivah. The next day, I spoke about reckless driving again, and I could see that my words hit home. There's nothing like a real-life demonstration to drive home the point.

Unfortunately, I have seen too many real-life demonstrations of beautiful homes wrecked beyond recognition by money disputes. I wish you would take my word for it and never have to witness such terrible tragedies.

I will grant you that you must take money into consideration in today's society. But it must never be allowed to become a point of contention. Letting the money bug into your home can only lead to tragedy.

— *18* —

*Security
Measures*

Dear Daughter,

Think back to when you were a young girl. Do you remember how you used to laugh when I told you I was a multimillionaire? You would look around our modest home and ask me where I kept my chauffeur-driven limousine and my private jet.

But now that you are a mature woman with your own home and children, I'll tell it to you again. I am a multimillionaire, and so are you. Am I wrong? Am I living in a fantasy?

I don't think so.

Let's go back just one or two hundred years in history. Let's consider for a moment the life of a rich man, even a very rich man, in the early 19th century. By what standards was he considered wealthy? So we'll make a list.

He had plenty to eat and drink.

He had plenty of nice clothes to wear.

He had plenty of coal to keep his house warm in the winter, although he couldn't do much to keep his house cool in the summer.

He had plenty of kerosene to keep his lamps lit in the dark.

He had a well in his front yard and an outhouse in his back yard.

He had a coach and a team of fine horses in his stable.

He could hire musicians to play for him when he needed cheering up.

He could afford to give his children a good education.

What else? Can you think of anything else? I'm sure I missed one or two things, but you get the idea.

Now, let's compare my life or yours with the life of that rich man. We are not lacking for food or drink or clothing. I doubt if that rich man had clothes any finer than those beautiful dresses your little girls were wearing last Shabbos.

We heat our homes with oil or gas and never have to shovel coal into the furnace. We flick a switch here and there, and our homes are flooded with light. We have air conditioning, running water and indoor plumbing, luxuries that are beyond that rich man's wildest dreams.

We don't need horses or stables, because even the most modest car will carry us across great distances more easily and more quickly than kings traveled in earlier times. And if we need to, we can hop onto a plane and fly anywhere in the world. Before long, it might even be within everyone's reach to hop onto a space shuttle and fly to the moon. Don't laugh.

What if we want music? We need only choose from countless inexpensive music CDs with outstanding acoustic quality. We have telephones, computers, fax machines.

As for education, it has never been better or more universal.

Face it. Those of us living in the developed countries enjoy an unbelievably rich standard of living.

So I was right, wasn't I? I really am a multimillionaire. If I had lived 100 years ago, I would have been the envy of the world.

Yes, I know exactly what you are going to say. What does life in the 19th century have to do with us? We are living right now, and that's all that matters.

But does it really? Am I supposed to measure my own situation by comparing it with the situation of others around me? Just because others may have more than I do, does it mean than I am not immeasurably blessed?

So you see, my dear child, I am indeed a multimillionaire. I live a very rich life, and so do you.

I hear your next questions coming. If we are all so rich, why are people under such constant stress? Why are they so tense and worried all the time?

The answer was given to us by King Solomon (*Koheles* 5:9), "Whoever loves money never has enough money." The desire for money is like a black hole. You feed it and feed it, but it is never filled.

A glutton who craves food can eat and eat and eat, but there is a limit. There comes a point when his gluttonous hunger is sated, and he cannot eat any more. But this is not the case with someone who is money hungry. There is absolutely no limit to this craving. The hunger is never satisfied. A person who loves money is always hungry. Always.

Let me tell you another of my little stories. When I was a teenager back in Argentina, I volunteered to raise some money for an important charity. In Buenos Aires at that time, there lived a very rich man who had business all over the world. In fact, he never spent more than two weeks of the month in Argentina. This man was known as a miser, and people had given up asking him for charitable donations. He never gave.

Being a brazen youth, I decided to try and get something out of this man, but how? Then I had a brainstorm. I would not ask him for a contribution, which he would undoubtedly refuse. Instead, I would ask him for a loan of a larger sum of money to be repaid in one year. A large loan would be very helpful to the charity, and I felt I could prevail on the rich miser to agree to it. After all, he wouldn't be parting with his money forever. In one year, they would be reunited.

Sure enough, the man agreed to lend me the money. He gave me the amount in pesos, the currency of Argentina, and I promised to repay the full amount in one year.

During that year, the peso fell slightly vis-à-vis the dollar, and by the time I repaid the loan the following year, the value of the pesos I returned was $100 less than the value of the pesos I had borrowed.

The miser was infuriated. "Look at what happened," he shouted at me. "I lost money on this loan. Don't bother ever asking me for a loan again."

I was mystified. Here was a man who routinely conducted major transactions worth millions of dollars. He regularly accumulated and salted away vast amounts of money. And here this same man was immediately aware of the slightest implications of currency fluctuation, and he was fuming over a paltry differential of $100. It was as if a great tragedy had befallen him. He made me feel as if I had caused him to lose his last hundred dollars. How could such a thing be?

Whoever loves money never has enough money. That is the answer. This man was not posturing. He was really and truly distressed by that $100 differential. He was not putting on an act. No, he was expressing the profound truth of King Solomon's words. If a person loves money he is always hungry for it. To that man, the loss of that $100 was like having bread pulled out of his mouth.

So now you are beginning to gain an insight into the obsession with money that has so deeply infected the society in which we live. Of course, not everyone is a miser, but almost everyone is focused on money. People have nice houses, with good heating in the winter, cool air conditioning in the summer and all the other comforts and luxuries that we all take so much for granted.

But if they are missing a certain thing they desire, they feel as ravenously hungry as a starving man who has not eaten for three days.

Why is this so?

It is because of the rush-hour syndrome. You never heard of the rush-hour syndrome? I'm not surprised. It is, you see, one of my own theories.

Imagine yourself strolling along a boardwalk in the cool evening breeze. All around you, other people are also enjoying leisurely walks. A relaxing scenario, isn't it? Now imagine if you would be taking the same leisurely stroll in midtown Manhattan during rush hour. People all around you are hurrying, running, the expressions on their faces intent and determined. Do you think you could continue that stroll with the same ease and relaxation?

Not very likely. Rather, you would begin to feel somewhat energized and driven in spite of yourself. Because that is human nature. The attitudes of the people around us are contagious.

If the people all around us are intent on accumulating more money and more luxuries, then we also tend to incline that way — unless we make a conscious effort to resist. And if we care more about our domestic harmony than the gratification of ever increasing desires, we have no choice but to make that effort to resist.

The Gemara (*Bava Metzia* 59a) tells us that "strife in the home is caused by financial issues." The commentators explain that actual shortages do not necessarily cause strife. Rather, it is anxiety about financial matters that disrupts the husband-wife relationship and destroys domestic harmony.

Financial issues play a major role in a marriage. They can trigger tensions, friction and misunderstandings, and they cannot be ignored. But what is the best way to deal with them? It is not to buy lottery tickets and run around in desperation in search of additional funds. These avenues will not solve the fundamental problem.

The solution is to reach down deep inside yourself and find the *bitachon*, the trust in Hashem, which will calm your soul and let you live through your situation with inner peace.

If husband and wife face their problems without *bitachon*, they will inevitably become motivated by self-interest and egotism. But if they face their problems with *bitachon*, they will be drawn together in their common faith. Whatever crisis they face will bring them closer together rather than drive them farther apart.

Years ago, the child of a friend of mine fell critically ill. When I visited them in the hospital, my friend told me with great emotion, "This has been a difficult time for us, but it has brought my wife and me much closer to each other. We strengthen each other in our *bitachon* all the time."

The Vilna Gaon points out that the first letter in the Torah is the letter *beis* of *bereishis*. This letter stands for *bitachon*. *Bitachon* is the starting point of the Torah, and it is also the starting point of the joy and harmony that you and your husband will enjoy together for the rest of your lives.

Dear Daughter,

So you want to know how we find *bitachon*. Do we just decide to have *bitachon*, and poof, we have it? Good question. I wish it were that easy.

I once read an article written by a famous professor of obstetrics. He presents himself as an atheist and goes on to describe all his high-risk experiments on the leading edge of scientific research. He delves into the deepest mysteries of life. But still, he sees no reason to accept the existence of Hashem. And then one day, he listens with his stethoscope to the heartbeat of his own child in the womb and declares, "There really is a Creator of the Universe. I believe it!"

How strange. What compelling evidence did he discover when he listened to the heartbeat of his infant child that suddenly convinced him there was a Creator?

I thought about this for a while, and I believe I have the answer. If a person observes the world from a purely intellectual perspective, he can see the most wondrous phenomena and still remain unmoved. Somehow, he will manage to explain away and rationalize everything he sees. He can listen to the heartbeats of thousands of infants and remain the same atheist. But when he hears the heartbeat of his own child, he is also engaging his emotions, and that changes his entire perspective. Suddenly, he sees with perfect clarity that only the Creator can transform a tiny speck of protoplasm into a living, breathing, thinking human being.

This, my child, is the gateway to *bitachon*. Think about the world with an open heart, and you will recognize the infinite greatness of Hashem. You will understand with perfect clarity that Hashem is in complete control of absolutely everything and everyone, and therefore, you will become convinced that there is no need for worry and anxiety. The Master of the Universe is holding you gently in His hands; how can you be more secure?

Let me tell you a little parable. The head of an orphanage traveled to Germany with the intent of visiting Baron Rothschild and asking him for a new building to house the poor orphans.

When he arrived, he went to the *shul* to pray. After *Shacharis*, he circulated among the prosperous-looking congregants and asked them for donations to the orphanage. The people responded kindly and generously.

Before he left the *shul*, he asked a man if he could tell him how to find Baron Rothschild.

"But you've already met him," said the man. "That gentleman over there who just gave you a nice donation, that is Baron Rothschild."

Now, my dear daughter, what would you say? Did the head of the orphanage really approach Baron Rothschild or did he

not? True, he spoke to him in the flesh and received a nice donation from him. But was that really an encounter with Baron
Rothschild?

I would say it was not. When you meet one of the richest
people in the world, you don't ask for a donation. You ask for a
building!

The same applies to our encounters with Hashem. The Gemara
tells us that Chanah, when she prayed for a child at *Mishkan Shiloh*,
used language that acknowledged Hashem's mastery over all the
host of the world, language she had never used before.

At that moment, the moment she stood in *Mishkan Shiloh*, she
was so inspired that she experienced a transcendent awareness of
the greatness of Hashem. This gave her prayer a new dimension
and made it effective. With her sudden insight that she stood in
the presence of the One Who possessed unlimited mastery of the
universe, she could ask for anything.

When you are in the presence of Baron Rothschild, you ask
for a building. But when you are in the presence of Hashem, you
ask for a child to be born from a barren womb. Nothing is beyond
His power.

The Midrash tells us that a Jew wonders (*Tehillim* 121:1),
"From where will my help arrive?" And he answers his own question, "My help is from Hashem." But that is inadequate. Hashem,
therefore, finishes the sentence for him, "The Maker of heaven
and earth." If you really, really grasp that I am the Maker of
heaven and earth, only then can you be secure in placing your
trust in Me.

That is how we open the gateway to *bitachon.*

A man once came to me for advice on strengthening his
bitachon. He was about to undergo a very serious operation, and
he was frightened. I found it very difficult to find the right words
to say to him, but we did speak about the issue of *bitachon* at
great length.

The operation was successful. I visited him when he came
home from the hospital, and he greeted me excitedly.

"You know," he said, "I was saying *Tehillim* in the hospital, and suddenly, I realized that King David was talking to me. Everything he said went straight into my heart and gave me strength. When he speaks of the incredible greatness of Hashem and his absolute trust in Him, I felt *bitachon* taking root in my own heart."

My child, should you ever encounter financial problems, I want you to view them as a gentle push from Above, as a kindly reminder to renew your relationship with Hashem.

Say *Tehillim* together with your husband. Let the words sink into your hearts. When both of you open your eyes and your hearts wide to the recognition of Hashem as the Master of the Universe, your home will once again become a peaceful and secure haven, an island of joy and serenity.

Dear Daughter,

I'm glad you liked what I wrote in my last letter about looking at the world with both your mind and your heart. But you still want something more practical. I sometimes forget how practical women really are. I think that's very good, because it takes a concept out of the realm of the abstract and makes it real.

Did I ever tell you about the American Jewish army officer who entered the camps with the liberation forces after the war? Stop me if you've heard this one before.

One day, two young boys approached the Jewish officer and asked him for a pair of *tefillin*. The officer had an extra pair, and he gladly gave it to them.

A short while later, the officer noticed the boys from the corner of his eye. They seemed to be playing some kind of game with the *tefillin*.

"Boys," he told them, "*tefillin* are not toys. They are not meant for playing."

"Sir, we are not playing with the *tefillin*," one of them replied with wounded dignity. "We have grown up in the camps, and no one has ever taught us how to put them on. We were trying to figure it out by ourselves."

My dear daughter, when we try to figure things out by ourselves we very often end up playing meaningless games. We need to be taught. We need practical direction.

Rabbeinu Yonah writes that even if a person is a true believer in Hashem he still needs to be trained to have *bitachon*. How do we understand this?

Let me tell you what I think. When I was a child in Argentina, there was an amusement park not far from my home. It was somewhat of a wild place, and religious Jewish children didn't go there. But we passed it very often, and I found it fascinating.

Most of all, I was captivated by a runaway train that passed through a dark and scary house making noises that foretold an imminent crash. I could hear the people screaming with fright as the train screeched and skidded to a grinding halt. When the train came back to the loading dock, the people got off with happy looks on their faces, and other people took their seats and prepared to scream with their own fright.

What was going on here? No one was really afraid of a crash, because they all paid money for the privilege of a seat on this train. In fact, they really enjoyed the delicious terror. And yet, when the train seemed to be about to crash, they screamed with genuine fright. Why?

Obviously, fear is a reflexive response. The mind may know there is no danger, but the gut is wrenched nonetheless.

This explains what Rabbeinu Yonah is saying. A person may be a true believer in Hashem, but he will instinctively react with fear. And if he allows this to go on for a long time, that fear will slowly but surely undermine his faith. Therefore, it is important that he be trained to have *bitachon* and overcome his fear.

So how do we train ourselves? The Midrash provides the answer. Before Queen Esther went in to see Achashveirosh, she was in a quandary. He hadn't called for her in 30 days, and it was against the rules to come uninvited into the presence of the king.

And so she prayed to Hashem, "...And You, O Father of orphans, please stand by the right side of this poor orphan who trusts in Your kindness. Let me find favor before this man, for I fear him..."

Look carefully at her words. Don't you see a contradiction? Here she says she trusts in Hashem, she has *bitachon*, and then she admits to fearing Achashveirosh. If she has *bitachon*, why is she afraid?

The Midrash continues with the story. After she finishes praying, she goes into Achashveirosh's inner courtyard. Achashveirosh reacts to this unexpected intrusion with a flash of anger. Esther sees his reaction and faints to the ground.

Once again, is this a person who has *bitachon*? Why did she faint from fear if she indeed trusted in Hashem? Did this show a loss of *bitachon*?

Absolutely not, says the Midrash. Quite the opposite is true. Hashem "responded to the anguish of the orphan who trusted in Him." He saved her from Achashveirosh's anger because of her *bitachon*! How did she display *bitachon*? By fainting?

If we look into the Midrash, we discover that while she was falling down in a faint she turned her head to the right and prayed silently to Hashem. She may have felt the instinctive emotion of fear, she may have been terrified to the point of fainting, but she never despaired. She never gave up. With her last ounce of strength, she turned to Hashem for help. This is *bitachon*. The fear did not drive her away from Hashem. It brought her closer, because she used it as a stimulus to pour out her heart to her Father in Heaven, to tell Him that she trusts in Him and Him alone.

If you and your husband ever encounter fears or worries about financial matters or anything else, use them as a stimulus. Grasp the opportunity to turn to Hashem with an overflowing heart, and tell Him that you place your trust in Him.

Condition yourself to do this always, and you will find your *bitachon* growing ever stronger. Despair and insecurity will fade into a distant memory. You will tell Hashem about the fear in your heart. Then you will look at your husband and your beautiful children, and you will be thankful for all the blessings He has showered on your home.

* * * * * * *

Dear Daughter,

Some years ago, a family in a certain American city lived in extreme poverty. The father worked very hard but earned very little. The mother struggled to stretch their few dollars as far as they would go, but the children still had to forgo basic necessities.

One day, the father called a family meeting.

"It disturbs me," he said, "that we have nothing put away for an emergency should we ever have one, Heaven forbid. So I have opened a bank account, and every week, I intend to put in something, even if it is only a dollar or two. At least, we'll have a nest egg, something to fall back on a rainy day. I want everyone to agree that the money can only be touched in case of dire emergency. Is everyone agreed?"

The children all nodded gravely. They would not pressure their father to dip into the savings. It was for emergencies only.

The years passed, bringing many trying times for the family. On more than one occasion, the option of dipping into the savings was discussed. Each time, however, it was agreed that they would somehow manage to get through their current crisis without compromising the family savings. It was important to leave the nest egg untouched. It was the family security.

Many years later, after the children were all grown up and married, they asked their father to reveal to them how much money had accumulated in the savings account.

"What savings account?" he asked.

"The one we scrimped and scrounged for all those years," they said. "The one we never touched."

"My dear children," he said, "there never was a savings account. I never had a single penny to spare, let alone a dollar or two. I made up the story of the savings account in order to give you all courage and a sense of security so that you would be able to cope with our poverty."

An amazing story, isn't it? It just goes to show you that people need to live with hope for the future. They need to know there is something on which they can fall back.

Well, I ask you, which is a more reliable source of security, a bank account or the power of Hashem?

For us, there is absolutely no question. Hashem is our banker, our insurance company, our guarantor of security. If we trust in Hashem, we can enjoy a serene, dignified and secure life.

But we have to make *bitachon* part of our lives. The Shelah writes that even a poor man who barely has enough to eat should set his table as if for a big feast.

Why? Because a person with true *bitachon* knows that Hashem is all-powerful, that everything can change in an instant. One day, a man can be impoverished and the next day he can be on top of the world. Everything is in Hashem's hands.

Strange as it may seem, the father who convinced his family that there was a substantial bank account gave them the gift of security. Time and again, they agreed to deprive themselves rather than dip into the phantom bank account. But their sense of security remained intact, because they believed they had something on which to fall back.

The poor man who sets his table for a feast also shows that he lives with a sense of security, only it is a real rather than an imaginary security. Even though he lives in poverty, he is secure in the knowledge that he is always in the hands of Hashem who will not abandon him. By setting his table he shows that just as Hashem decided to put him in a position of poverty, He can just as easily move him into a position of riches at any moment He so chooses.

I want to leave you with an interesting parable by which the Rishonim taught the concept of *bitachon*.

A poor man used to walk through a very affluent neighborhood every day on his way to work. One day, he saw a construction crew break ground on a new building site. As the days passed by and turned into months, the poor man saw the foundation laid and the structure begin to rise.

It was a magnificent structure, unlike any the poor man had ever seen in his entire life. It sprawled across a hilltop, and its soaring roof seemed to touch the sky. The sunlight reflected off its numerous windows, and the white marble walls gleamed like jewels.

As the building took shape, however, the poor man became annoyed. The builder had apparently made a glaring error. In the middle of the front wall, the builder had left a huge gaping hole. How could he do such a thing? fumed the poor man. Had he run out of marble?

Every day, the poor man passed the new building and saw the jagged gap in the front wall, and every day, his distress grew. How absurd to construct such a beautiful edifice and leave a hole right in the middle of the façade!

One day, he saw a crew of workers bring a golden frame and fit it right into the gap. The poor man was intrigued. What could be the purpose of this frame?

The next day, another crew brought an enormous sheet of glass and placed it into the frame. The poor man stared at the sparkling window that had suddenly appeared right in the middle of the façade. He had never seen such a huge window, and he would never have imagined that such windows existed. But there it was, a veritable crown jewel, a vision of extraordinary beauty offering panoramic views to the residents within and a visual delight to the world outside.

Now the poor man understood. The builder had not made any mistakes. It was the poor man himself, with his limited knowledge, who had made the mistake.

All of us are just poor people who cannot fathom the plans of the Master Builder of the Universe. We see the magnificent beauty of His structure, and we also see elements that appear to us as flaws. We cannot understand why this calamity or that problem should mar the exquisite symmetry of the world. Why should the marble walls of our lives have gaping holes in them?

But if we truly trust in Hashem, if we have real *bitachon*, we can feel secure in the knowledge that the Builder has no intention of creating anything less than a perfect masterpiece. If we are patient and do not despair, we will eventually see the crown jewels that fit into those spaces we once considered gaping holes.

— *19* —

The Safety Valve

Dear Daughter,

On my last trip to Buenos Aires, I met a friend of the family who had fought in the Falklands War. The Falklands is a group of islands about a thousand miles off the coast of Argentina in the South Atlantic Ocean. It is a British possession, but the Argentines also claim ownership over the islands, which they call the Malvinas.

Because the islands are so much closer to Argentina than to Great Britain, the Argentines believed they could take it by force, and so they invaded and seized the islands. There was euphoria in Argentina, but it was short lived. A short while later, the British fleet arrived, and the British forces landed safely on the islands.

At that point, it was all over. Argentina's untrained army was no match for the military might of Great Britain, and prudence would have dictated that they immediately sue for peace. But they did not. They continued to fight desperately even though they had no prospects of victory, and in the process, thousands of men lost their lives.

This friend of the family had fought in the war, and he remembered the fighting with bitterness. He told me that during one battle a soldier carrying a new assault rifle asked him, "My friend, could you tell me how to operate this weapon?" Incredible!

Thousands of men died because their leaders allowed them to become cannon fodder. It was like a mass suicide.

"I don't understand," I said to our friend. "Why didn't they negotiate a peace? Why allow thousands of men to die for nothing?"

"Pride," he said. "Plain and simple pride. Argentina had worked itself into a nationalistic and patriotic frenzy, and the leaders were too proud to back down and sue for peace. So for this all those thousands of hapless men had to give their lives."

On my way home, I thought about this a long time. It was overwhelming. What a destructive force pride is! How irrational it is! There is no end to the damage it can cause in relationships, in a marriage, in just about anything.

Shortly after I returned home, I saw something equally incredible right in my own *shul* on Yom Kippur.

There were two families in our neighborhood, whom I will call the Kalischmans and Yefimovitchs. Blood enemies. They had been friends at one time, but then there was that notorious scandal, which we will not mention here. From then on, they were at each other's throats for years. Not speaking is only the least of it. They both accused each other of every crime and misdeed conceivable. I shudder just to write about it.

Well, on that Yom Kippur I was sitting in the *shul* saying *Tefillas Zakah* quietly, when suddenly I hear an outburst a few rows behind me. It sounded like heavy weeping. I felt a little self-conscious about turning around to see who it was. Perhaps the man would be embarrassed. But as the weeping persisted, I could not help turn around to look. Who knows? Someone might need help.

Do you know what I saw? Mr. Yefimovitch was asking forgiveness of Mr. Kalischman for suspecting him of something which he had not done. Both men were weeping profusely as they embraced each other.

At that moment, I offered up a silent prayer of thanksgiving to Hashem for giving me the privilege of being part of the Jewish people. The stiff pride of the Argentines would not relent under the most withering British fire until thousands of men lay dead on the killing fields. But we Jewish people are taught to overcome our pride and do what is right. It must have been hard for Mr. Kalischman and Mr. Yefimovitch to swallow their pride and make up, but they did it. And it was a true *kiddush Hashem*.

How fortunate we are to be Jewish! How fortunate we are to be conditioned by the Torah to overcome pride and face up to the truth.

⌒―

Dear Daughter,

As you know, Mr. Kramer, who lives down the block, owns a whipped-cream factory. One day an Italian engineer came to see the plant. As Mr. Kramer was showing him around, one of the pressurized pipes burst, and a shower of whipped cream shot forth. Within a matter of seconds, however, one of the workers had shut the main valve. The whipped-cream shower came to an abrupt end.

"I am impressed," said the Italian engineer. "Back in Naples, it would have taken a half-hour before anyone thought of shutting the main valve. By now, we would all be covered in whipped cream. You are certainly more efficient than we are. But we have more fun."

Mr. Kramer thought this was a very funny story.

Why am I telling it to you? Because it came to mind when I was thinking about safety valves. Any time pressure builds up, it is important to have a safety valve to release some of that extra pressure so that you don't have an explosion.

In a whipped-cream factory, the pressure build-up can result in a drenching whipped-cream shower for everyone in the vicinity if the safety valve isn't turned off. Some people may find this annoying, and some, like the Italian engineer, might find it fun. There is no accounting for tastes.

But when pressure builds up in a domestic situation, no one in the world would think that the explosion will be fun. Unless the safety valve is turned off quickly, it can only lead to serious trouble.

In the factory, we know where the safety valve is. It is clearly marked "safety valve."

But where is the safety valve in a domestic situation? What do you do to release the build-up of pressure when tensions rise in the home?

Very simple. The safety valve consists of two little words: "I'm sorry." If you must swallow your pride, as the Torah teaches us, and say, "I'm sorry," the situation will instantly improve.

Even if you believe very strongly in your position, the tension usually arises not from what you said but how you said it. If the way you spoke hurt your husband's feelings, then you should apologize for that, and vice versa of course.

Once tensions subside, you can deal with your issues calmly and intelligently.

Remember! At the first signs of tension, reach for the safety valve. Say, "I'm sorry." Don't wait for the field to be strewn with casualties, like those Argentine generals in the Falklands.

Don't fall victim to your own vain pride. Turn instead to your Jewish pride. Remember that the Torah wants us to admit our errors and ask forgiveness.

Find within yourself the courage to say, "I'm sorry," in the midst of a heated argument, and you will really have something special of which to be proud.

❧

Dear Daughter,

No matter how many times I read the story of Joseph and his brothers in the Torah I am always deeply moved. The scene which touches me the most is the reunion.

After 22 years, the brothers finally meet again. This time they are not the self-confident sons of Jacob who condemned their younger brother and sold him into slavery. This time they stand as humble supplicants before their long-lost brother who is now viceroy of Egypt.

Such high drama, such pathos, such a turnaround. Can there ever be a reconciliation? Can these estranged men become brothers again?

Joseph wanted a reconciliation, and so he spoke to their hearts. He reassured them that his being sold into slavery was all part of the Almighty's master plan, that it was all meant to be so that he would be in place to take care of his family during the great famine.

But all this was to no avail. It was as if a great iceberg separated Joseph from his brothers, and their hearts remained filled with fear and shame.

How did he finally break through to them? How did he finally melt that iceberg? Rashi explains that he cried. Joseph's hot tears melted the iceberg.

What was behind those tears? I saw in a *sefer* that it was an acknowledgment by Joseph that he shared in the guilt of his brothers. He was also partly to blame, for he had spoken *lashon hara* against them. For 22 years, he lived with the knowledge that he had brought this retribution upon himself, and now that knowledge resulted in an emotional outpouring to his brothers. This is what finally melted the iceberg between them and brought about their reconciliation.

Joseph could have set himself up as a prosecutor against his brothers. He could have confronted them with what they had done and forced them to beg forgiveness. But he chose not to do so. He chose to take some blame upon himself, and this was what brought the brothers back together again.

My dear child, what you would have done in his situation? Would you have been the stern prosecutor holding their feet to the fire in righteous indignation? Or would you perhaps have had the courage to shed tears of contrition for your own share of the blame? Knowing you, I expect you think you would have risen to the occasion and done what Joseph did.

Well then, let us relate the same situation to your marriage. Let us take a hypothetical situation. Your husband does or says something that hurts you. He is clearly at fault. How do you react? Do you become the relentless prosecutor, proving to him beyond a reasonable doubt that he had been terribly inconsiderate and that he should be ashamed of himself? This may help you restore your self-esteem, but will "putting him in his place" restore a harmonious balance to your marriage? Unlikely.

On the other hand, you can melt the iceberg by acknowledging that you are also a little to blame for what happened, which is usually the case in such situations. A few tears of contrition on your part, and your husband will undoubtedly admit his guilt as well. And you know what? That iceberg will dissolve in an instant!

By the way, don't think for a moment that I am saying this only to you and not to your husband. The exact same thing applies to him. Both of you have to find it in yourselves to acknowledge your guilt in order to ensure that your marriage will always be harmonious. Ah, but it so hard to do. Sure, it is easy to say, "Swallow your pride and apologize." But when it comes right down to it, how do you do it? Let me give you a hint.

Do you remember that Argentine soldier I told about a few

letters ago, the one who fought in the Falklands War? Here is another story he told me.

Etiquette is viewed strictly in the military. A soldier is required to salute any officer who outranks him, and Heaven protect him if he should fail to do so. He can get into really big trouble.

One day, my friend was absorbed in what he was doing, and he barely noticed that someone was passing by.

"Private!" a harsh voice rebuked him. "Why don't you salute?"

My friend looked and nearly fainted dead away on the spot. Standing before him with his hands on his hips was the general of the base. Belatedly, my friend managed a stiff salute. With bated breath, he waited for the general to announce the severe punishment that was undoubtedly coming his way.

"At ease, soldier," the general suddenly said, and he smiled. "Don't worry, I won't punish you. But be more careful in the future. I may let this pass, but you can be sure no junior officer would let it pass. Forget to salute one of those people, and you will really be punished!"

A very illuminating story, wouldn't you agree? Why would a general overlook a soldier's transgression of military etiquette but not a junior officer?

The answer is very revealing of human nature. A general feels very secure in his rank and honors, and therefore, he can afford to be magnanimous. A junior officer always feels insecure about his rank, and therefore, he insists that others always pay him the proper respect.

I believe that both you, my daughter, and your wonderful husband are generals on the domestic front. Both of you have so many qualities and such exemplary characters. Therefore, you can both find it within yourselves to rise above petty pride and admit your share of the guilt should there ever be any friction. Remember, it takes greatness to forgive, but it takes even more greatness to ask forgiveness.

— 20 —

She's His Mother

Dear Daughter,

When you first got married, I worried about so many different things. How would you get along with your husband? How would you adapt to leaving the home in which you grew up? How would you deal with the responsibilities of running your own home?

Do you know what I worried about the most? You'll be surprised. I worried about how you would get along with your mother-in-law. Unfortunately, all too many people have problems with their mothers-in-law, and I was afraid that you might be among them.

Thank Heaven, it turned out that you have a truly wonderful relationship with your mother-in-law, and I'm sure the credit goes to both of you. But I would still like to discuss this critical issue. You never know when a situation may arise that might cause tension between the two of you, and a few advance words of advice from your father might help you avoid a serious problem. Besides, among your many friends there might be some who do not get along with their mothers-in-law. Perhaps you can pass on my few humble opinions to them.

Let me begin by saying that getting along with your mother-in-law is fundamental to your happiness. She is your husband's mother, and he undoubtedly loves her. If you do not get along with her, it will be a thorn in the side of your relationship with him. This is a fact.

Nonetheless, animosity between wives and mothers-in-law is also a fact, one of the more miserable facts of life. Our Sages (*Yevamos* 117a) acknowledge this unfortunate reality. It is also the subject of much mean-spirited low humor. People laugh, but they cringe within.

Why is it so? Who knows?

One thing I can tell you for sure. It doesn't have to be that way. I know countless people who have wonderful relationships with their mothers-in-law, including you, my own wonderful daughter. These people are the most fortunate of the fortunate. They never have to lower themselves to squabble in the gutter, and in their home, they enjoy harmony and bliss. Very wise.

To some people, getting along with their mothers-in-law may be the most natural thing, but for others it must be quite an ordeal.

So what are they supposed to do if they rub each other the wrong way?

The answer is entirely in the mind. Imagine for a moment that a mother has a child running a very high fever. She calls the doctor, and instead of asking her to bring the child into the office, he offers to stop by on the way home. He comes into the house and examines the child, and out of his concern, he sits up with the child all through the night until the crisis passes.

How would that mother feel towards that doctor? Gratitude is a pale shadow of a word to describe her feelings. He will forever be a knight in shining armor to her, no matter how distasteful she may find his choice of clothing, manners and personal habits. Nothing matters. He will always be the one who tended to her child through the long hours of the night. He can do no wrong.

Well, think for a moment about what your mother-in-law has done for you. How many nights did she drive sleep from her eyes to stay up with her darling little boy when he was sick? How much blood, sweat and tears did she expend on her little boy until he became the fine young man that he is today, your own wonderful husband?

Believe me, she did far more for you than that doctor did for our imaginary mother in distress. In your eyes, therefore, your mother-in-law should always be a (figuratively speaking) knight in shining armor. This woman's heroic efforts brought you the fine young man who is now your husband, and therefore, she can do no wrong.

Aha! I can hear you taking a debating stance. I know exactly what you are going to say. The doctor did it consciously for the mother and child, but your mother-in-law was not thinking of you when she stayed up nights with her son. That's what you are saying, am I right? Of course I am. I stayed up plenty of nights with you, and I know you quite well.

But you are mistaken. When a person harvests his field, the stalks he forgets to take go to the poor people, and the Torah tells us that he will be blessed for it. Our Sages further deduce that a person receives blessings if he accidentally loses a coin and a poor man finds it and feeds his family with it. Do you see? Even if he had no idea that he was providing dinner for the poor man's family, it counts to his credit. Certainly your mother-in-law deserves the credit for every bit of good that was derived from all those nights she stayed up with her son, from all the effort she put into him.

Remember also that this wonderful husband you so love and admire is the product of the upbringing he received in her home. Whatever shortcomings she may have — and who doesn't? — she molded your husband into what he is, and you must be forever grateful.

The Sefer Hachinuch writes that it is impossible for a person ever to repay his parents for what they did for him. Besides everything else, they gave him life! Well, your mother-in-law gave your husband life, and indirectly she gave life to you and your children. How can you ever begin to repay her for that?

I once heard a story about the Chasam Sofer. Someone had done something terrible to him.

"What bad thing or good thing did I ever do to him that he should hate me so much?" he wondered aloud to one of his disciples.

"I don't understand," said the disciple. "A bad thing might cause him to hate you, but a good thing?"

"It's really quite simple," said the Chasam Sofer. "When you do a person a good turn, he can no longer be neutral to you. From then on, either he loves you, or else, if he cannot find it in himself to love you, he will find a reason to hate you. Neutrality is impossible."

I think that this may account for some of the resentment to mothers-in-law. A wife has received so much good from her husband's mother that she can never be indifferent to her. She must either love her or resent her. The wise, high-minded wife finds it within herself to love her mother-in-law, while the foolish, small-minded wife resents her.

Think about it. Everything depends on your attitude and perspective. If our imaginary mother could look up to the doctor unquestioningly despite all his faults and shortcomings, a wife can certainly do the same for the woman who gave you the most precious gift in your life — your husband.

Dear Daughter,

You ask a good question. Okay, so you have the right attitude and perspective. You appreciate that your mother-in-law gave life to your husband and brought him up, and you are grateful. But how does a wife deal with the day-to-day irritations that might come up in her relationship with her mother-in-law?

The answer is respect. The Shelah writes that "a wife must respect her husband's parents even if they are vulgar people." People can train themselves to behave with respect, and when they do, their entire outlook changes. If a woman trains herself to be respectful to her mother-in-law at all times, she will find that those little irritations you speak about will disappear.

I was once visiting a yeshivah, and I overheard a boy say to his friend, "You know, the cook is a Nazi."

Understandably, I was shocked. "Excuse me, young man," I said. "I hear what you just said. Why do you call the cook a Nazi?"

"Because he gives small portions and refuses to gives seconds."

"And for that he is a Nazi?"

"Of course."

Incredible!

I did not pursue the conversation any further. But I'll tell you one thing. If that boy had been taught to behave with respect to his elders, he would never have called that cook a Nazi. What's more, it would never have crossed his mind to compare his yeshivah's cook to a Nazi.

A prominent *rav* once told me that a certain girl, whose name he did not mention, consulted with him regularly about her personal problems. Eventually, her frustration led her to forget herself and speak sharply with the *rav*.

The *rav* rebuked her for speaking with disrespect and explained to her that no matter how difficult things were, she should always be respectful. The girl, who was really a very fine person, was properly chastened, and she immediately apologized with full sincerity. She promised to work seriously on being respectful. Amazingly, her problems began to disappear within a few weeks. Her new attitude had helped her see the world from a different perspective, and things were not so bad.

This is the key to getting along with a mother-in-law. Number one, she deserves and should be given absolute respect. With that taken care of, everything else should fall into place.

A young man once came to me with a terrible problem. His mother had come to visit for a week, and while his wife was out shopping, his mother had gone through all the drawers in the house. His wife discovered what had happened because she had a very distinct way of arranging her drawers. She immediately saw that they had all been disturbed, and no one else had been around.

"Did you ask your mother about this?" I said.

"I did," said the young man ruefully. "She admitted it. She said she just wanted to see if everything was in order."

"And what does your wife say?"

"My wife thinks my mother is a monster, that she is beneath contempt. And what can I say? My mother is really a good, well-meaning person, but can I defend what my mother did? I can't, because I think it was terribly wrong."

"It definitely was," I said.

"So what can I do? I feel that I am trapped between my mother and my wife."

I thought about this problem for a few minutes.

"Tell me," I said, " where is your mother now?"

"She went home."

"When will she be coming back?"

"In about two months."

"Will you be seeing your wife's parents in the meantime?"

"We will be visiting them next week."

"Good. This is what I want you to do. When you are with your wife's parents, treat them with great respect. And make a point of it to see that your wife notices. Afterwards, speak to your wife very openly. Tell her that just as you are making an effort to treat her parents with exceptional respect, she should do the same for your parents, no matter what she feels inside. Tell her that your mother is really a good person, but she is just a human being, with virtues and faults, just like everyone else. Ask her to give your mother respect simply because that is what the Torah demands. Ask her to do it for you. I'm sure she will. Let's see what happens."

I also told him to speak to her regarding the points I made in my letters to you on the topic. Had the situation been at a further stage of deterioration, I would have recommended that they go to see an *adam gadol*. But at this early stage, I felt my simpler remedies might still help.

Two weeks later, the young man called to tell me that his wife had agreed to behave with respect, although she still harbored deep resentment to her mother-in-law for what she had done.

Three months later, he called me again. The most miraculous thing had happened. His mother had admired a certain dish in their china closet. His wife filled the dish with fresh-baked cookies, gift-wrapped it and gave it to her with a card. On the card she wrote, "A small gift from me to the person who gave me the greatest gift in the world." Later, she told her husband that she had forgiven his mother and accepted her for what she was. He should relax. Everything was fine.

An amazing story, isn't it? But it is 100 percent true.

This wife is truly a person to be admired. She was able to overcome her resentments and make peace, a tremendous accomplishment at any time. But more than that, I admire her cleverness. She understood that only by making real peace with her mother-in-law could she preserve the perfect love and beauty of her wonderful marriage.

⌒

Dear Daughter,

Children grow up with an idealized vision of their parents. They are larger-than life-heroes in their eyes. Parents are the ones who anchor and stabilize their world, who provide for all their needs, who know the answers to all questions, or at least most of them. Therefore, when a child see a shortcoming in his mother he will instinctively downplay it so that it will not interfere with the image he has conjured up in his own mind.

Mothers-in-law never get the benefit of the doubt. Most people are so predisposed against their in-laws by the snickering jokes and widespread cynical attitude of the world at large that they immediately think the worst.

It is the wise woman who appreciates the importance of having a good relationship with her mother-in-law, who will keep an open mind not only regarding her own mother but also as far as her mother-in-law is concerned.

This we find in the Torah itself, in the Book of *Ruth*. After the death of her two sons in the land of Moab, Naomi returned to Israel, accompanied by her two daughters-in-law Arpah and Ruth. Both of these women were Moabite princesses, and both were prepared to endure the privations of poverty and displacement in order to be with their beloved mother-in-law. And yet, when Naomi asked them to turn back, Arpah returned home.

What did Naomi say that convinced Arpah to leave?

The Midrash tells us that Naomi said, "I am punished because my sons married you," meaning non-Jewish women, in violation of the Torah. Arpah immediately interpreted these words as a personal rejection. All the love she had felt for Naomi went up in smoke, and she spun on her heel and left.

Ruth, however, listened to Naomi with an open mind, and she understood that her words were sad and full of love. Therefore, she remained by the side of her mother-in-law. Eventually, she bore the future Davidic dynasty of Israel and became one of the most honored women in Jewish history.

Dear Daughter,

One last word on the subject of maintaining a good relationship with your mother-in-law. It comes with another one of my stories.

A young man I know once called me with a problem he was having at home. He wanted to go to his parents for *Yom Tov*, but his wife didn't want to go. Could they come over to talk to me?

An hour later, they were sitting in my dining room.

After the pleasantries, I asked his wife why she didn't want to go.

"Because it's *Yom Tov*," she said. "I don't want to seem mean, but I work very hard all year, and I look forward to *Yom Tov* as such a special time. I just can't spend it with my mother-in-law. She makes me so uncomfortable. I'll gladly go there for an ordinary visit. But not *Yom Tov*. That is too much."

I considered her words thoughtfully. "I hear exactly what you are saying," I finally said. "It is a difficult thing. Let's leave this topic for a while. You are an intelligent young woman. I have a question to ask you."

"Of course," she said.

"I am going to tell you a story about two young people who have been dating for a while. Everything seems perfect. They go on a special date, and she feels sure he is going to propose to her. He does propose, but he adds one condition. She must agree never again to step into her mother's house. Now what do you think? Should she accept the proposal on that condition?"

I cannot describe to you the look of shock on that young woman's face. "Accept it? Accept it?" she spluttered. "That's the most disgusting thing I ever heard. She should tell him good-bye and never talk to him again. That what she should do! The nerve!"

I nodded. "I quite agree with you," I said, "but let me ask you another question. Is what you are doing to your husband really so very different from what this hypothetical young man was trying to do?"

"What do you mean?" she asked, genuinely puzzled.

"How do you think your husband feels?" I asked her. "You are basically telling him that he can never again step into his mother's house on *Yom Tov*. This is his mother we're talking about. He loves his mother. Every man loves his mother.

"I once heard about a great *gadol* who was sitting *Shivah* for his mother. The people that came to pay their respects commented on the good fortune of this woman to have left behind a son with so many honorable titles. The *gadol* burst into tears. 'But I have lost the title "my dear son," which only my beloved mother bestowed on me.'

"A mother is irreplaceable. Do you understand? And what you are doing is removing your husband's mother from an important part of his life. All those memories of his home during the wonderful *Yom Tov* times, that's what they will all have to remain. Just memories. The reality is being cut out of his life. With what will you replace it? Let me tell you, nothing replaces a mother."

The young woman looked at me with tears in her eyes. It was clear that she had never thought of what she was doing in the way I was portraying it.

"So what do you think I should do?" she asked.

"Go there for at least part of the *Yom Tov*," I said. "And make an effort to get along with your mother-in-law. Be gracious. In your own mind, remind yourself that you are doing this for your marriage, so that your beautiful relationship with your precious husband will not be harmed. Is this too high a price to pay? I think not.

"If things do not go exactly as you want them to, consider that life is not perfect and that the situation is only temporary. It will pass in a few days, but your relationship with your husband will be with you every day of the year for the rest of your life. Between you and me, you may very well discover that, when you come to terms with the situation, spending a few days of *Yom Tov* with your mother-in-law is not nearly as bad as you thought."

One Plus One Equals None

Dear Daughter,

I think I'm basically coming to the end now, and I would like to conclude with a very serious subject.

In our day and age, we are so exposed to the gentile culture that it is almost impossible not to be influenced. Many of their attitudes and perspectives are unfortunately popping up even among our own people and causing great damage.

So how do we protect ourselves? The first step is to recognize what is Jewish and what is not.

With issues of modesty and the like, this is not too difficult. But when it comes to social issues and attitudes about family life and children, believe me, it is an altogether different story.

Let us begin with the Jewish view. What is the main purpose and goal of a marriage? According to us, it is to build a Jewish home in which the Name of the Creator will be sanctified and in which proper Jewish children will be raised. The marriage certainly has to address the needs of husband and wife. That is obvious. Otherwise, it simply wouldn't work. The Sages tell us that a man should give more honor to his wife than he seeks for himself. If he has only one egg, he should give it to her and eat plain bread himself. But that is not the central, overriding purpose of marriage.

In the Torah view, when a man and woman marry, they form a partnership with the Creator. From that point on, their first concern is to fulfill the objectives of the partnership. Before they can worry about their own particular needs, they need to make sure they are fulfilling their responsibilities to their Divine Partner. And what are those objectives, those responsibilities? One of the most important ones is to bring children into this world and raise them in the way of Torah and *mitzvos*, the perpetuation of *Klal Yisrael*.

What an awesome responsibility! Can you imagine a general on the battlefield being concerned about personal matters? Impossible. Only after the battle is done can he allow himself the luxury of thinking about himself. The same applies here. A Jewish father and mother must focus on their primary responsibility, which is raising good Jewish children, before they can think about themselves. Unlike the gentiles who believe in "ladies first" or "me first," we believe in "children first."

And you know something? More often than not, this intense focus on the needs of the children brings the parents closer together.

Not long ago, I attended the *bar-mitzvah* of a Down syndrome child, and it left a deep impression on me. I have, *Baruch Hashem*, attended numerous *bar-mitvahs*, and invariably, the parents glow with happiness. But I have never seen a father as radiant with joy as the father of this particular boy when he managed to recite a short but complete *bar-mitzvah* speech.

It must have been very hard to prepare this child for his *bar-mitzvah*, not to mention the years of struggle and heartache that led up to it. Well, let me tell you, when the boy finished his speech and the people shouted out their *mazel tovs*, I saw the boy's father and mother exchange a glance that was so eloquent and so touching that tears sprang to my eyes.

The glance proclaimd pride in each other, mutual esteem and respect, intense devotion. It revealed the golden bond that united this man and this woman. They had struggled side by side, enduring the pain and the joy together, giving each other constant encouragement and support, and here were the results. Together, they had scaled a high mountain, and now they stood together on the mountaintop. Do you see what I am saying? By giving so much to their child, they were themselves immeasurably enriched. This is the Jewish way.

In the gentile world today, however, there is an entirely different perspective on marriage. People get married for purely selfish reasons. They want security, companionship and any number of other benefits they can derive from the state of marriage. This sort of marriage is also a partnership, but only between the man and the woman. And what is the objective of this partnership? It is basically a deal. You give me what I want, and I will give you what you want. Two selfish people scratching each other's backs! And where do children fit into this picture? You guessed it. Children are just another of their selfish needs, another of the adornments that will be added to this marriage as it goes along. New car. New house. New children. Pretty much in this order of priority.

But what happens when the stresses of life begin to tug at the relationship between husband and wife, as they always do? Once again, the selfish considerations come to the fore. Husband and wife deal with their marital problems when and where it is convenient and expedient. Their battles so often spill over into the central arena of the home, because keeping the children insulated from the marital stresses is not a primary concern. After all, the children are no more than by-products and bystanders, and they must go with the flow.

Eventually, the frictions between the couple may lead to separation. And why not? The marriage was created to serve their selfish needs, and it is no longer accomplishing that. There is an old saying that "you can't argue about taste." This husband and wife are no longer to each other's taste, and it is time for a parting of the ways.

But wait a minute, you protest. What about the children? Ah yes, how unfortunate. The children will undoubtedly suffer, but what can be done about it? It is all just a terrible accident. The suffering of innocent bystanders.

Aha! There's that word again. Bystanders. Because that is exactly what they are. Bystanders. The children were always secondary in the marriage, and now that it is crumbling, it will not be maintained for them. The parents have a right to get what they are seeking from life, and the poor children are the tragic victims of cruel fate. They will just have to learn to deal with it.

You shudder, my dear daughter, as well you should. You know, I am reminded of an article we once read together a long time ago. Do you remember the story of the mother whose teenaged son was stricken with polio? If you don't, let me remind you. One fine day, this mother rented a furnished apartment, deposited her crippled son together with his wheelchair in the living room and gave him an envelope filled with cash.

"My son, you are on your own," she said. "You now have an apartment and a substantial stake of money. I wish you the best of luck in life."

Then she turned and walked out of his life. Just like that. After all, she had a right to live a normal life, didn't she? I remember how you fumed when we read that article. What kind of mother is this who would abandon her own child? You were furious, and I was very proud of you.

Well, how about parents who set their own selfish interests before the needs of their children, who fight in front of them and

cripple them emotionally? Are they any less guilty of abandonment than the mother who left her polio-stricken son to fend for
himself?

In my opinion, the increase in marital problems and even
divorce among Jewish families is a direct result of the insidious
penetration of the gentile outlook into our community. It sounds
so natural to look out for one's own rights and needs, doesn't it?
But in a Jewish marriage, it is selfish and wrong. Our own rights
and needs are secondary to the rights and needs of our children.
We come together to bring them into this world, and we stay
together to give them the stability and security that will allow
them to grow up happy and productive members of the Jewish
community.

My dearest daughter, if you are ever inclined to lash out at
your husband in the presence of your children in immediate
response to something he said or did, hold yourself back.
Remember who you are! You are a Jewish mother, entrusted
with that holiest of missions, the upbringing of young Jewish
children. No matter how strong your pain and aggravation,
clamp your lips shut before any angry words burst forth. A
quick angry response may give you momentary relief and satisfaction, but think of what it will do to your children. It will
scar them for life. Make the sacrifice for the sake of your children. Never fight in front of them. It is a sacrifice you will never
regret. I promise you.

$\backsim$

Dear Daughter,

Last time, I wrote to you about the terrible effects of fighting
in front of the children, comparing it to the abandonment of a
crippled child. So why does it happen? Don't people realize what
they are doing to their children by letting them witness friction
between their parents? You are probably thinking that such par-

ents must be cruel and heartless people. Unfortunately, it is not necessarily so.

Let me tell you a story. Many years ago, before air travel became so common, I traveled from Argentina to Israel by ship. It was a beautiful experience, the peace, the vastness of the boundless ocean, the stunning sunrises and sunsets. But there was no kosher food served. It took three weeks for the ship to reach Italy, and for all this time, I had to subsist on little more than fruit and crackers.

When we reached Italy, there was a layover of a few days, which we spent in Milan. In the freezing cold, I set off in search of a Jewish family who would offer me some hospitality and a hot meal. As I was walking through the streets, a man with a black hat approached me. I won't tell you his real name, so we'll just call him Mr. Levy.

"You look lost," he said. "Can I invite you to my home?"

I hesitated for a moment.

"Don't worry about a thing," he said with a kind smile. "We have *glatt kosher* right here in Milan. We'll take good care of you."

I was so happy I almost hugged him right them and there.

The Levy home was a truly wonderful place, a typical observant island right in the middle of Milan. The Levys were indescribably kind and considerate to me. They had a little baby girl named Linda who gurgled and cooed happily while we sat and conversed.

All through the evening, I kept wondering why they were being so nice to me. My Italian was poor even then, and I thought I must be missing something they were saying, something that would give me a clue to their exceptionally solicitous welcome to a young stranger from halfway around the world. What did they have up their sleeve?

But as the evening wore on, I came to the realization that they expected nothing from me. They were simply wonderful, kindhearted Jews. Nothing more, nothing less.

Many years later, a young couple came to me with a tale of woe. She introduced herself as Linda Kagan, the daughter of Mr. and Mrs. Levy of Milan. She remembered that I had been in their home so many years before, and she felt she could turn to me as sort of an old friend of the family.

The young couple had been married for 15 years, and they were having severe problems with their children. I spoke to them for a while, and they impressed me as very fine and considerate people.

We made an appointment to meet a second time. The second time, the husband was called away, and the wife came alone. We spoke again, and my sense of puzzlement returned.

"Tell me," I said, "would you mind talking about your childhood and your relationship with your parents?"

She hesitated for a moment, then she nodded. Clearly, I had touched a raw nerve.

"If you don't mind," I prompted her.

"Of course," she said and drew a deep breath. "My parents are very special people. Everyone holds them in the highest regard. I am very proud of them."

"That's good. Your parents, did they get along well with each other?"

Her eyes opened wide. She tried to speak, but couldn't. Instead, she burst into tears. I was very embarrassed, but I said nothing. I just waited patiently for her to regain her composure and say what she wanted to say.

"I can't believe it," she finally said. "Oh, may Hashem forgive me. I didn't realize. I really didn't."

"What didn't you realize?" I asked gently.

"When I was a young girl, I remember one evening sitting in the kitchen with my mother. After a while, my father walked in, and my parents started arguing. I don't remember what they were arguing about, but I remember that their words were very angry and bitter. My mother lashed out at my father and belittled him right in front of my eyes.

"'Mother, please,' I pleaded, 'please don't say these things. I don't want to hear them. Is this the way you want me to treat my future husband?'

"My mother gave me a cold look and continued where she had left off, completely absorbed in her anger and impervious to my tears. I ran from the room. The memory has remained buried all these years, but now it comes back. How dreadful! And what's worse, I've been doing the same thing to my own children. Oh, Heaven forgive me. What have I done?"

What can I tell you, my dear daughter? It just didn't make sense to me. How could it be possible that those incredibly kind and hospitable people would be so nasty to each other in front of their children? And yet, it was true. Tragically true.

We spoke for a long time, and I gave her encouragement to deal with her situation, to try to make amends at this late date. For hours after she left, I couldn't think of anything else. How could such a thing be? To say that her mother had been blinded by anger was simply an inadequate excuse. It doesn't explain her behavior.

And then it struck me. She had undoubtedly rationalized her behavior. She had absorbed the "me first" ideology, and this helped her rationalize her priorities in marriage. Her first consideration was her own needs, not the child's. She was convinced she was doing the right thing, even if her little girl didn't understand, even if her little girl felt her world crumbling around her. Rationalization is a dangerous thing.

I read an article about a study conducted in the Jewish community about the incidence of child abuse. The centerpiece of the article was an interview with a man who had beaten his 10-year-old son so severely that he had to be hospitalized with broken bones and bruises over his entire body.

"How could you be so brutal to your own child?" he was asked.

"I am responsible for the education of my child," he replied, "and I take my responsibilities very seriously. Children must be obedient and respectful to their parents. And if they are not, they must be disciplined. Sometimes, they have to learn the hard way. Of course, when a parent gives medicine to his child he sometimes gives a little too much. An overdose is a freak accident, a human error."

The article goes on to report that these freak accidents occurred with alarming frequency. How could a Jewish father be so cruel? There is only one answer. Rationalization. This fool convinced himself, in order to cover up his own inner rages, that it was his obligation as a father to educate his son by means of regular beatings.

Fighting in front of the children is also child abuse, leaving psychic scars that are often deeper than physical ones. How does such a thing happen? Rationalization. People convince themselves that their first responsibility is to themselves, and the consequences to the children are secondary, a freak accident.

Not so, say the Sages. In a Jewish marriage, the children are always first. The main purpose of the marriage is to bring children into the world and bring them up properly. When husband and wife accept this, they will find that any tensions and frictions that arise can be overcome, and that the relationship forged between them in such a setting is more powerful and satisfying than a relationship based on selfish needs.

Let me just conclude with another story.

A number of years ago, a young man came to ask me for advice about certain marital problems he was having.

"I am kind of embarrassed to tell you what we fight about," he said. "They really are pretty minor issues. You know, like who gets the car and when, who does what around the house, small things like that. But it's what's behind these things that really gets me down. We're really not getting along. It just takes one tiny little spark to set things off all over again, and then we're at each other's throats as usual."

"I see," I replied. "Of course, you are careful never to fight in front of the children, right?"

"Well, you know how it is. I try my best, and I suppose my wife does, too. But sometimes it just can't be helped, you know?"

"No, I don't know. There is no excuse for fighting in front of the children. Absolutely never."

The young fellow shrugged. "I guess. Anyway, we've gone beyond that. The situation at home is really unbearable, and it looks like we're headed for divorce. I want to talk to you about it."

"About what?" I asked. "Divorce? Positively out of the question! How could you even think about it?"

This was not exactly what he was expecting to hear from me. "Out of the question?" he spluttered. "Why? It's just not working. Sometimes, you just come to a parting of the ways, if you know what I mean."

"All I know is that you have children," I said angrily. "How could you contemplate divorce with young children at home? Do you know what divorce would do to them?"

"Yeah, it's a bummer," he said. "But what can I do? I have no choice."

"What do you mean you have no choice? You certainly do have a choice. You can stay together and work it out for the sake of the children."

"Without meaning any disrespect, rabbi," he said, "you live in a sheltered yeshivah world. You're not in touch with the real world."

By the way, did you notice that anytime someone tells you they don't mean any disrespect, you can be sure something disrespectful is coming your way? And when they tell you they don't mean to be difficult, you can be sure they're going to be difficult? Anyway, on with the story.

"Oh really?" I said. "And what goes on in the real world?"

"Today, people who don't get along don't prolong the agony. If it doesn't work, they get divorced and go their separate ways. It's tough for the children, you can't deny that. But things work out for everyone. The parents usually remarry, and the children end up having two homes, two sets of parents, two birthday parties or *bar-mitzvah* parties. It's life, that's all, and you go with the flow. It's as simple as one plus one equals two."

What can I say, dear daughter? I just sat there with my mouth agape. The naiveté, the callousness, the utter foolishness. I have to admit I found myself at a momentary loss for words. What could I say to this fellow that would turn him around? Then I had a flash of inspiration.

"Wait here one minute," I said. "I want to show you something."

I ran down to the basement and rummaged around until I found what I was seeking. It was an old Gemara.

"Here, this is it," I said as I walked back into the room.

The young man looked at the Gemara doubtfully. "You're going to show me a Gemara? Something that says you can't get divorced?"

"Not quite," I said. "You know how boys often doodle on the inside covers of their Gemaras when they're bored or distracted? Well, those doodles are very revealing. Sometimes, you look at some of those scribbles written almost subconsciously, and you get a very good idea at what's going on inside the head."

"Okay," he said. "I'll buy that. I know what you're talking about."

I opened the front cover of the Gemara and showed him what was written there. "Here, read it aloud."

"One home," he read, "plus one home equals no home." Then he gasped as the full import of what he had just read sank in.

"That's right, my young friend," I said. "This Gemara belonged to one of my *talmidim*, a boy from a broken home. One of those lucky enough to have two homes, according to your way of thinking. Well, he didn't quite see it your way. In his mind, he had no home. Are you prepared to do this to your children? Think about it."

Well, I'm glad to tell you that the young man went home and had a long talk with his wife. They agreed that divorce was not an option and that they would do everything they could to work out their problems.

Last week, this couple made a *bar-mitzvah*, and I made sure to attend. It was such a beautiful sight to behold. The boy was beaming through and through. And the parents? Well, it was pretty obvious they had recaptured what they had enjoyed with each other in the early days of their marriage.

My dear daughter, I'm not telling you these things because I suspect that, Heaven forbid, they apply to you directly. Since you brought up the topic, I'm taking advantage of the opportunity to air my views and put them down on paper. You've always been my best listener.

In any case, perhaps these dreadful stories that I witnessed with my own eyes will make you think twice before you say anything in the least bit caustic to your husband in the presence of your children. Also, if you would impress these things on your friends and neighbors in that special, diplomatic way you have of getting messages across, you would be doing everyone a great favor.

Especially the children.

* * * * * * *

Dear Daughter,

Just the other day I heard an interesting story that relates to the matters we've been discussing, and I thought I'd pass it along to you.

An old acquaintance of mine, a well-known psychiatrist from England, recently paid me a visit and related a very disturbing encounter he had with one of his patients. This is a real case history, but I will disguise the names of the people and some other details that might give away their identity.

The Weiss family — how's that for a common name? — lived in the Golders' Green section of London. Mr. Weiss made a decent living, and the family lived in a respectable house in a nice neighborhood.

At first, Mr. and Mrs. Weiss got along reasonably well, despite Mr. Weiss's somewhat difficult nature. Two things bothered Mrs. Weiss about her husband. One, he was very frugal. She called it stingy. Two, he demanded that his wife prepare everything for him exactly to suit his fastidious tastes. Nonetheless, Mrs. Weiss made the best of it, and the family flourished.

As the children began to grow up, however, serious frictions began to appear in the marriage. Mrs. Weiss insisted her children be dressed in the very finest clothes, but Mr. Weiss stubbornly refused to pay the price. As the couple fought more and more, Mrs. Weiss stopped catering to her husband's finicky tastes, and this only made matters worse between them.

They decided to seek professional help and went to see my psychiatrist friend. He spoke to them at length about learning to accept each other's shortcomings. He also warned them against fighting in front of the children.

"I understand you want your children to be dressed nicely," he told Mrs. Weiss. "But tell me, is it worth crippling them emotionally for life?"

"Do you think I'm heartless, doctor?" she replied. "Believe me, I love my children dearly. But I'm also a person. I also have to live, and I tell you I can't stand living with a miser!"

"A miser!" Mr. Weiss exploded. "That's easy for you to say. You don't have to slave all week long to put food on the table. You don't appreciate financial responsibility. You just want to spend, spend, spend."

"Say what you want," she shot back. "We both know what you are. A miser! Miser, miser, miser."

He glowered at her and turned away, refusing to say another word. And so the session came to an end. Miserably. The situation at home continued to deteriorate, and presently, they came to a meeting of the minds. They would seek a divorce.

Mrs. Weiss called her children together to tell them the news.

"Your father and I have reached a decision," she told them with tears streaming down her cheeks. "We are going to get a divorce. You have all seen how difficult things have become at home. Quite unbearable. Sometimes, we just have to face reality and make the tough decisions. You know, not every shoe fits every foot. The same holds true with people. Not all husbands and wives fit perfectly together. And when it gets too painful, you just have to do what you have to do." By this time, the children were bawling openly.

"I know it's going to be hard, children," she said, weeping herself. "We'll just have to be strong. Look at your friends. Quite a few of them have parents who've divorced. They've made it through all right. We will, too. We'll just have to keep a stiff upper lip!"

Well, I don't know about stiff upper lips, but things did not work out so well for Mrs. Weiss. Oh, she got her divorce and rid herself of her troublesome husband, but the problems with her children started almost immediately. They became sullen and withdrawn at home, and their grades suffered terribly. One of the boys became a serious discipline problem at school, and he was expelled from one yeshivah after another.

Mrs. Weiss became very resentful of the Jewish community for not being supportive enough and helping her deal with her problems. Being an articulate woman, she actually wrote a book, titled *I Am a Jewish Child*, in which she takes the community to task for its failures and demands that an educational program be instituted to address the special needs of children such as hers.

When the book was published, it caused quite a sensation, and she took advantage of the publicity to promote her cause. The excerpts I will soon quote are verbatim, straight from the book.

Late one night, she came home to find one of her sons sitting on the living room floor and reading her book. Curious to see his natural reaction, she was careful not to make a sound so as not to announce her presence. The boy seemed to be enjoying the book, but suddenly his face became distorted by rage. He slammed the book shut and stormed from the room.

Shaken, she went up to her room and straight to sleep. In her dream, she heard a loud knock at her door. The door swung open and a stern-faced rabbi in a long black coat and a black hat handed her a piece of paper. "You are summoned to the court of our master, the Chafetz Chaim!" he declared. Then he spun on his heel and walked out.

The scene immediately shifted to the study of the Chafetz Chaim. The great sage, his face glowing like the sun, sat behind a rickety wooden table piled high with *sefarim*. He nodded at her, then he turned to his attendant. "Let the accusers enter."

To her surprise, her eldest son entered. He was covered with bruises and hobbled with a cane, so crippled she could barely recognize him. She felt a knife twist in her heart.

"Rebbe, years ago I was a happy child," he began. "I was full of life and joy. But now I am no better than a cripple, the victim of the battle between my parents. I have no day, no night, no Shabbos, nothing, only shame. How I envy the orphans. At least, they have no shame!"

"This is a serious accusation," said the Chafetz Chaim. "Do you have any proof?"

"I most certainly do," said the boy. He took out a copy of his mother's book. "This book was written by my mother. It is called *I Am a Jewish Child*. I am going to read word for word from page 57. It reads as follows: You have to understand these children. They go to *shul* and sit alone on the bench, envying any child that is sitting happily beside his father. 'Why am I different?' he says to himself. 'Because I come from a broken home. What a shame! An orphan at least has pride in the wonderful father he once had. People remind him of it. But me? Everyone looks at me like a *nebach*.' This is how these children feel.

"When these children come home," he continued to read, "they take out their homework sheets with a picture of a father making *Kiddush*. But where is his father? Making *Kiddush* for someone else! Instead of his father standing at the head of the table, his mother sadly makes the *Kiddush* for them. 'Why am I different?' the child asks himself. 'Is this what a Shabbos should be?' Yes, you must understand these children to know how to deal with them."

The boy closed the book and began to tremble. "Rebbe, do I have the right to call myself a cripple? Am I not a cripple?"

After the boy finished speaking, the Chafetz Chaim sat with his head down for a few long minutes. Finally, he lifted his hand to the heavens. "Hashem," he pleaded, "give me the strength to bear so much suffering."

The boy left the room, and her second son came in. He was dressed like a bum from the street.

"Why do you dress like this?" asked the Chafetz Chaim. "Is this the proper attire for a good Jewish boy?"

"Do you think I dress like this because I want to be a bum?" the boy replied. "No, Rebbe. In those days when I had a happy home, my dream was to be just like you. You were my role model! But then the troubles started, and I lost respect for everything and everyone. I accuse my mother, and I accuse my father! Doesn't the Torah say that children should not die for the sins of their parents? Well, I am no better than dead because of the sins of my mother and father."

"These are serious accusations, my child," said the Chafetz Chaim. "Do you have any proof?"

"Yes, I do." He opened a copy of his mother's book. "I am going to read from page 36. It reads as follows: Sometimes these children react by rebelling. They are so sad, so full of shame, that a tornado of rebellious emotions spins them around to seek the company of the dregs of society."

He closed the book. "Rebbe, I accuse my father and mother. They snuffed out my Yiddishkeit!"

The Chafetz Chaim wrung his hands. "Hashem, Hashem, give me strength to bear all this suffering."

The boy left, and the mother remained standing in her place, trembling uncontrollably. Her book lay on the table, accusing her silently by its very existence.

"Mother of these children," the Chafetz Chaim said to her, "you have heard the accusations of your sons. You have heard the proofs they brought from your own writings. Now the time has come to confess your sins. It is the first step. Say it aloud. Repeat after me. 'I have sinned. I was cruel to my children.'"

When she heard these words, she burst into tears. "But I wasn't cruel," she screamed hysterically. "I am a Jewish mother. Would I be cruel to my children?"

The Chafetz Chaim took her book in his hands. He opened it and leafed through the pages until he reached page 83. He began to read. "*Roshei yeshivah*, principals, teachers and the whole community should feel the plight of the mothers of these children. Their tragic suffering is so great. First they suffer from the failure of their marriages, and then they must endure all these difficulties alone."

The Chafetz Chaim read the last few sentences again and again, each time stopping on the word "failure." The frightened woman cringed inside.

"Mother of these poor children," said the Chafetz Chaim, "were the first years of your marriage happy?"

"Yes," she replied, her voice almost inaudible.

"And when you started having trouble, were you warned not to let your arguments spill out into the open?"

"Yes," she replied in a hoarse whisper.

"When your friend was injured in a car accident, did you berate her for not wearing a seat belt? Did you call her irresponsible for not doing what she could to prevent injury?"

"Yes, I did."

"Well, did you do everything in your power to prevent the emotional injuries of your children?"

"No, I didn't," she whispered.

The Chafetz Chaim banged on the table until it shook. "The Torah demands that your first concern be for your children. A little patience, a little sacrifice by both you and your husband, and your children could have been happy today. If you had only resisted the impulse to fight all the time, even in front of the children, you could have saved your marriage. You and your former husband are responsible for what happened to your children."

She broke down in tears. "What can I do?" she wailed. "Oh, what can I do? I have sinned. Tell me, Rebbe. What should I do?"

"Listen to me," said the Chafetz Chaim. "Just as you made it your crusade to get the community to understand the plight of children such as yours, you must now make it your crusade to prevent these things from happening. You must speak to friends and neighbors about the horrendous effects of fighting in front of children. Write books and articles. Speak in public. Speak in private. You can save hundreds of children from the pain and suffering you visited on your own children. That is what you must do."

The Chafetz Chaim's room faded away, and Mrs. Weiss was instantly awake. She had broken out in a cold sweat, and her heart beat wildly.

She slept no more that night, and she was already waiting for the psychiatrist when he arrived at his office.

After listening to her story and doing whatever he could to help her, the psychiatrist wrote an article about it in one of the Jewish publications of the city. It caused quite an uproar in the community.

Now, dear daughter, I'm not saying this dream, or rather nightmare, was a Divine revelation or anything of the sort. But I believe it showed that, deep down, Mrs. Weiss knew she had done the wrong thing by her children, and she felt guilty about it. This is what came out in the dream.

I believe most people understand themselves how terrible it is to fight in front of the children. The trouble is that people lose their reason when they get angry. They do cruel and irresponsible things in the heat of the moment, and when the heat finally dissipates, they may find it is too late and their families are in ruins.

This is what you should impress on your friends and your neighbors, my dear daughter. Let it become fixed in their minds long before any trouble may start, Heaven forbid, that no matter what happens, the children must be protected. They must never be subjected to the agony of seeing their home go up in flames right before their very eyes.

Yes, dear daughter, if only we would be guided by the ideals of the Torah rather than selfishness, we would all be much happier.

Especially the innocent children.

My dearest daughter, I hope that you have gained as much from these letters as I have and that together, I as the speaker and you as the listener, we have created a work that will bring a little more peace and harmony into Jewish homes everywhere.

I give you the blessing of a loving father that you and your husband should always respect and cherish each other, that your home be sanctified by the love that will reign between you always.

Appendix

Focusing on the Children

Dear Daughter,

In our earlier exchange of letters, we've discussed thorny issues that can affect the marital relationship, such as money, family and different customs. But there is one issue which is perhaps more important than all the rest. It comes up every single day and is so close to your hearts that it is impossible not to be affected by it. I am talking about your children.

Children can be the source of our greatest joy, but they can also be the cause of our greatest pain and sorrow, Heaven forbid. Should problems with children ever arise, the tensions they create in a family setting are capable of inflicting the most terrible emotional injuries.

Therefore, it is critical that husband and wife work together, not only for the sake of their children but for their own sake as well, to develop a consistent and effective approach to child-rearing. In this way, they will be able to preserve the peace and harmony of the home and nip any incipient problems in the bud.

And should problems arise despite their best efforts, they will deal with them together, standing shoulder to shoulder as allies with one heart and one goal in mind, with love in their hearts for each other and for their children and a fervent prayer forever on their lips.

What I am about to write in these next few letters, my dear daughter, is not a guide to raising children. That is a very complex issue that needs to be dealt with at length. And you will often have to consult with *gedolim* and expert educators. All I can do here is give you some very general guidelines in a broad framework. I will rely on your and your husband's good common sense to know when you can deal with a situation yourselves and when you should seek help.

You know those home remedy books you have at home? Those are fine as long as the problem is not serious, but when you're running a high fever, you put away these books and go to the doctor. The same applies to raising your children. If a problem seems to be serious, don't deal with it on your own. Don't experiment on your own children. Get help.

In the meantime, let me present some basic ideas to you. One of the most difficult aspects of bringing up children is maintaining control through discipline. What is the best and most effective way to discipline children? A difficult question.

During my childhood, my parents hit me very rarely. My mother used to discipline me by withholding privileges which I wanted very badly. Believe me, it was effective. I was once at a friend's home, and I saw his father hit him for some misdeed. When I came home, I begged my mother to hit me when she wanted to punish me rather than withhold my privileges. So you see, parents have to decide for themselves which method of discipline will be most effective in a constructive way.

The Reishis Chachmah writes that parents should not exert too much pressure on children who have reached the age of adulthood, because doing so may cause them to rebel and sin against their parents.

The same holds true to a certain extent with younger children as well. Although they are less likely to rebel openly against their parents, too much pressure may plant within them the seeds of future rebellion.

On the other hand, discipline is critical, especially in our own times when the discipline and order of society at large has broken down to such a great degree. Today more than ever, the discipline a child receives in the home will determine the direction of his entire life.

So what are you supposed to do?

Let me tell you something that happened to me when I was only 6 years old. It was a very traumatic experience. In fact, even as I write about it now, I cannot help but wince.

You see, the pinky finger of my right hand got caught in a door, and the first joint was severed almost entirely. It remained attached to my finger by a slim sliver of skin. Our family doctor was about to sever this last connection and leave me with a truncated pinky finger, but my parents would not let him do it. Instead, they took me to a famous surgeon, a real specialist.

The surgeon used some innovative techniques to reattach my finger, and the operation was successful. While putting on the cast, however, he pressed so hard that I actually saw stars, believe it or not. I remember the pain as vividly as if it had happened just yesterday. The doctor explained to me that he had to do it in order for the finger to heal properly, and I accepted it.

I remember how fond I was of this doctor as a little child. It didn't matter that he had caused me tremendous pain, because I understood that it was completely for my own good. Because of him, I have a normal pinky finger on my right hand.

Having said this, let me now tell you about a Midrash. Our Sages tell us that a father who refrains from hitting his son is showing hatred for the child. Why? Because unless the child is disciplined, he may go astray. He will grow into an emotionally deformed person. On the other hand, a father who disciplines his son and hits him from time to time is showing his great love, because he is assuring that his son will grow up straight, emotionally stable and strong in his values.

You know, of course, that our Sages were extremely sensitive to the pain of a child. We don't recite the *Shehechianu* blessing at a *bris* because of the pain of the child. Certainly, they wouldn't take the matter of hitting a child very lightly, and yet, they insisted that a father must punish his child from time to time. Clearly, it is of tremendous importance.

So what are the rules and guidelines?

The fundamental rule is that punishment has to be completely for the good of the child, as a reinforcement for the lessons of the Torah. The child has to see that the parent is not hitting to vent his own anger but because he feels deeply about the importance of the *mitzvos* of the Torah.

I once read an article about a Jewish gangster in Chicago. His father had been shot in a gangland shootout, and he grew up on the streets, eventually joining a rival gang and becoming its leader. One day, as his gang prepared to execute an audacious robbery he had carefully planned, this Jewish gangster just got up and walked away from his life of crime.

What happened?

As he writes in the article, he remembered a scene from his early childhood when he had stolen an apple from a pushcart. His father sat him down on his lap. "The Torah says, '*Lo signov*, do not steal,'" he said in a tearful voice and he administered a slap to the boy. Two more times, he repeated the *mitzvah* of the Torah and the slap to the boy.

That morning, as they prepared to execute the robbery, this scene came back vividly to this Jewish gangster. He saw again the anguish on his father's face as it rose up before him, and he could not bring himself to go through with the robbery.

This father's hitting had been effective, because it was the right kind.

You know, I often notice how successful almost all parents are in keeping their children from running into the street. Almost invariably, they use a well-placed slap on the wrist to emphasize the severity of the matter.

Why is this more effective than other punishments?

The answer is very simple. When a parent punishes a child for running into the street, it is 100 percent clear that the punishment was administered purely for the benefit of the child. The child instinctively understands that he received the punishment because his parents were so very deeply concerned for his well-being and safety. Therefore, he has no problem accepting the lesson and obeying the wishes of the parent.

In other circumstances, however, it is not clear at all. When a parent punishes a child, it may sometimes be, at least in part, out of anger and frustration. Such punishment is worse than none at all. The child is very likely to resist the wishes of the parent, and in the process, he will have learned that his parents are ruled by selfishness and anger. It is a destructive lesson.

I was once visiting the home of a rich friend. We were sitting and talking in his cavernous dining room under an immense and very delicate-looking crystal chandelier. Suddenly, his two young sons came bursting in kicking a soccer ball from one to the other.

"Boys," said my host half-heartedly, "you know you cannot play soccer in the house. There are many fragile things around that could easily break."

The boys mumbled something and continued to play with the soccer ball. Clearly, these were spoiled children. My host did not seem to be getting anywhere with them.

I was thinking about what he should be doing in this situation when a loud noise disturbed my thoughts. One of the boys had given the soccer ball a particularly hard kick and it had flown up and shattered the chandelier. I looked around. There were glass slivers everywhere.

My host jumped out of his chair in a rage. He grabbed the young culprit and began to beat him so violently that his wife had to plead with him to stop. "You're killing him," she kept screaming.

Unfortunately, this is a scenario that we have all seen all too often, although perhaps not amidst such a spectacular display of shattered glass.

The truth is that it is sometimes hard to avoid this kind of angry reaction, even though we all know that it is destructive.

But there is a way to avoid it. The Vilna Gaon offers some extremely insightful advice on the matter. A parent should only hit a child because of the future, never because of the past. Corporal punishment should only be administered to prevent a recurrence of some unacceptable behavior. It should never be administered as punishment for past deeds.

If my host had conditioned himself to follow this sage advice, he would have taken a strong stance as soon as the boys appeared with the forbidden soccer ball. The boys would have related to it well, because they would have understood that their father was teaching them important lessons.

But that was not what my host did. He reacted only after the fact, venting his rage for what had already happened. The child did not see a parent teaching him important lessons in life. He saw an angry man lashing out at his son because a valuable object had been destroyed. The child feels hated and humiliated, and the only lesson he has learned is that adults react to stress with temper flare-ups.

Keep the words of the Vilna Gaon in mind, and you will be safe. Never hit a child unless you expect to accomplish something for the future of the child. You will be doing a favor for him and for yourself as well.

The Special Responsibility of the Mother

Dear Daughter,

Bringing up your children is one of the greatest joys imaginable in life, but it also come with great burdens. If you sometimes feel that the burden falls mainly on your shoulders, you happen to be right. The Reishis Chachmah writes that *tzaar gidul banim*, the pain and suffering of raising children, is borne mostly by the mother, and therefore her reward is very great if she fulfills her mission faithfully.

So now you know that it is not only you who feels the heavy weight of the burdens of raising children. It is the same with all mothers, because that is how Hashem made the world. Okay, so is that supposed to make you feel better?

Yes, it is. Because if Hashem gave you the heavier share of the burden of raising children, He undoubtedly gave you additional tools with which to accomplish your goals.

My dear daughter, you really have very special skills and talents for raising children. Do you know what they are? Let me tell you.

The Torah tells us, "Honor your father and your mother." Why does the Torah mention the father before the mother? Rashi explains that the Torah has to emphasize the importance of honoring fathers since children are naturally more inclined to honor their mothers. Why? Because she "wins them over with kind words."

Mothers have a special faculty for speaking directly to the heart of their children with gentleness and kindness, and the children respond. Harsh words are very painful to a child. They can cause serious damage, but kind words are like a balm to the heart and soul.

This is your special responsibility in the home. You have to win over your children with kind words and your own soft touch. That is not to say that your husband should be harsh to them while you are gentle. On the contrary, he should be as kind and gentle as he possibly can. But in the end, you are the one who has the greater natural skills, and therefore, you are the one who has the greater responsibility. And the greater reward.

I would like to add a small but extremely important point.

If you remember, a number of years ago Cabbage Patch Dolls were all the rage. Everyone just *had* to own one. This doll was not much to look at. In fact, it was quite ugly. It also didn't talk or do anything else.

What was so special about this doll?

Some marketing person thought of using computer technology to make each one different. And that was what was done. Each doll came with its own birth certificate and pedigree, and the buying public went wild. Some of the buyers even sent the dolls to nursery or day camp. Can you imagine such foolishness?

But under all the hysteria and the madness there is an important lesson to be learned here about human nature. There are billions of people in the world, and everyone is afraid of becoming just another number, a face lost in the huge mass of faces. The uniqueness of the dolls, therefore, appealed to their buyers because it struck a deep chord in their personalities.

Our Sages addressed this feeling. They tell us that each person is an entire world, that it would have been worthwhile to create the entire universe just for the sake of this person. Any person. Every single person in the world is special in his own way, and it is important that he know it. This is called self-esteem. When a person has self-esteem, when he is convinced of his own worth, he will be successful and fulfilled in life.

We live in a very stressful society. Great value is placed on excelling in school, and those children who simply do not have the skills are in danger of falling by the wayside. There are also many other areas where children may not measure up to preferred standards. But are these children less valuable, less precious in the eyes of Hashem? Of course not. Each and every one of them would be reason enough for the creation of the universe.

You, as the mother, with your special ability to touch the hearts of your children, must reassure them that they are unique and infinitely valuable. If you help them develop good self-esteem, they will be well prepared for life.

One last thought along these lines. You may find that your children, especially as they grow a little older, become less obedient. Although this is wrong, it is unfortunately nothing more than natural behavior. The natural tendency of a child is not to learn, not to pray, not to take on responsibility, not to do anything but indulge and gratify his desires. It is the task of parents to condition the child to do the right thing.

How can parents ensure that their children will accept their guidance? How can they ensure that their children will obey them?

Our Sages tells us that the key is to form positive parent-child relationships, to make sure that children genuinely like, admire and respect their parents. There is no question that the love of a parent for a child is boundless, that there is nothing in this world a parent would not do for a child. And yet, a child could easily ignore all the love and the sacrifice of his parents if he does not like their approach to the relationship. He may give them respect because he has to, but he will not be receptive to their guidance.

Parents sometimes feel that their children are part of them, like an arm or a leg, and they need about as much wooing and attention. But this is wrong. Children should never be taken for granted.

When I was a youngster back in Buenos Aires it was a very turbulent time. The trend among young people was rebellion against the older generation and authority in general. But I was never so inclined. I always treated my father with the greatest respect and obedience.

Do you know why? I'll tell you.

Every once in a while, my mother would be away from home at dinnertime, and it would be the responsibility of us men to fend for ourselves. Since we were only boys in the house, we all knew our way around the kitchen, and it was not particularly difficult for us to get our own dinners. But my father did not allow it. Instead, on those occasions, he insisted that he himself prepare dinner and serve it to us at the table as if we were the most distinguished guests.

I cannot begin to tell you how excited and pleased we were on those nights when my father would fuss over us. With a father like that, it would have been impossible not to like and admire him, and it would have been ridiculous to disobey him. In the same way, you as their mother can touch the hearts of your children.

Remember this: It is not necessary to give in to your children in order to have a good relationship. It is not necessary to become their slaves. But it is necessary to express your love to your children in a way that touches their hearts. If you can accomplish this, they will respect and obey you. I guarantee it.

Instilling Faith at an Early Age

Dear Daughter,

Now that we are on the subject of *chinuch*, raising Jewish children, I would like to discuss with you some of the most fundamental responsibilities of a Jewish parent.

I recently read a historical article based on a German language archive that had just been translated into Hebrew. It seems that many hundreds of years ago the Grand Duke of Austria tried to extort money from the Jewish community to help him pay for a war he was waging. He took 120 women hostage and locked them in his dungeon. The women remained in captivity for a long time, and they became convinced they would never come out alive.

One day, a message came that the women were to be expelled from the country. The women were relieved that they would at least escape with their lives.

Wagons arrived, and the women were transported away from the prison. The wagons did not go far, however. They brought the women to a field where stakes and pyres had been set up. The grand duke sat on his horse in full regalia, and glared at the Jewish women as they alighted from the wagons.

"You are all going to be burned alive at the stake," he said, "to avenge the death of our savior."

You can imagine the shock for these women. Here they thought they were being given a reprieve and allowed to live, and lo and behold, they are about to be burned alive.

The women looked at each other, and suddenly, they broke into a spontaneous dance.

"Do not be afraid," they reassured each other. "This world is but a dream. In a few minutes, we will all be with Hashem, enjoying everlasting life. We now have the opportunity to sanctify His Name. Come, let us dance for joy!"

And so, all of these women died with the words of *Shema* on their lips.

Do you know what I see in this story? I see much more than heroism. I see the fruits of an incredible *chinuch* deeply imbedded into their souls by generation after generation of parents who taught their children the most fundamental concepts of life. At the moment that these young women discovered they were about to die, it was of course a terrible shock to them. They were not expecting it, and therefore, they had no time to prepare themselves intellectually. They had no time to think. They could only react by instinct, and the way they reacted, therefore, revealed the profound *emunah* and *bitachon*, faith and trust, that existed in their inner core. To them, the concept of reward in the next world was a reality, a subject discussed so often in their daily lives that it was as real to them as the sky above.

Where does such a powerful *emunah* come from? Only from

the *chinuch* they received as children. Their parents undoubtedly impressed on them from the youngest age that there was reward and punishment in this world, that the good would go to *Gan Eden* while the evil do not. They sucked these concepts in with their mother's milk, and it became part of their very essence.

There is no other way to explain how 120 women faced with the shock of unexpected imminent death could burst into a spontaneous dance of joy.

Think about the story of Chanah and her seven sons, all of whom gave their lives rather than bow down to the king's idols. Even the youngest child, just a little toddler, refused to bow down. Not only that, but listen to what this child said.

When the king told him to bow down, he replied, "I am afraid of the Master of the world."

"Does the world really have a Master?" asked the king.

"Have you ever seen a world that has no owner, is neglected and runs by itself?" asked the child.

What a sophisticated response! For a toddler to be conditioned to think this way can only be the result of incredible *chinuch*. From the moment he could understand, this child was taught the concepts of reward and punishment. He knew to be afraid of the Master of the world. And for him to think in such sophisticated terms shows us the capability of youngsters to achieve a profound understanding of *emunah*, even at a very tender age — if they are taught correctly.

So what is the correct way?

Let me tell another of my little stories. It happened when I first came to Lakewood from Argentina. One day, after *Shacharis*, I went over to Rav Aharon Kotler *zt"l*, the Rosh Yeshivah of Lakewood, to speak with him.

During our discussion, he said to me, "The Targum writes that the voice of Hashem at Mount Sinai never stopped." He smiled at me. "So if it didn't stop, where is it? Where can you hear the voice of Hashem?"

I looked at him without answering. I didn't know.

He pointed to his Gemara. "Here," he said. "This is where you can hear the voice of Hashem."

I was too young at the time to understand the profundity of what he was telling me, but that finger pointing at the Gemara impressed me deeply. The concept stuck with me, and as time went on, I began to achieve a glimmer of understanding.

Why did it stick with me? Because I could relate it to something concrete, to that finger pointing at the Gemara. The idea had reality even though I didn't understand it.

This is a very important thing to remember when you are teaching a child abstract ideas. How do you give a child a strong belief in *emunah*? How do you get him to love *Gan Eden*?

You have to relate these concepts to something concrete. When the child tastes something delicious, tell him that it is nowhere near as delicious as *Gan Eden*.

Your child will also go very much by what he perceives in you. If you are emotional and sincere when you speak about the wonderful pleasures of *Gan Eden*, he will accept that as a reality. And he will be motivated to do more *mitzvos* and learn more Torah in order to achieve this wonderful thing called *Gan Eden*.

Let me also point out to you what the Rambam writes in his *Letter to Yemen*. "My brothers," he writes, "when you raise your children teach them about the gathering of the Jewish people at Mount Sinai. Speak about the greatness and splendor of this event in your public gatherings, for it is the pillar that upholds our faith and the pathway to the truth."

It is not enough for a child to believe in the giving of the Torah at Mount Sinai, to absorb it as a piece of information that is filed away with all the other information stored in his brain. This great event has to be integrated into the fabric of the child's life. The parents must talk about it again and again with excitement, as they would about a thrilling vacation the family had taken together.

The child must feel that scene come alive in his mind. He must feel the thrill of standing at the foot of the mountain together with millions of other Jews and hearing the voice of the Almighty with their own ears. He must feel that he himself has received the Torah, that he himself was commanded to do the *mitzvos* by Hashem. Talk about this with him constantly. It will become part of him, and his *emunah* will rest on a rock-solid foundation.

It is up to you and your husband to instill this powerful *emunah* in your children. It is the most important thing you can do for them to set them on the path of a true Jewish life. I hope that these few points I have raised will be helpful to you. There are, of course, many more ideas and methods for accomplishing this great goal. You and your husband need to discuss and study this question together.

Believe me, if the two of you make a concerted effort, you will transform the atmosphere in your home. You will be doing the greatest favor for your children.

And for yourselves as well.

The Importance of Demanding Respect

Dear Daughter,

One of the traits I have always admired about you is your humility. You don't seek honor or hunger after recognition. You are secure with your own worth, and therefore, you enjoy a serene life.

But I want to make sure your humility doesn't stop you from teaching your children the *mitzvah* of *kibud av va'em*, honoring parents, in its full meaning. Remember, the *mitzvah* is not for your benefit but for the benefit of your children. They must learn to be grateful, and to whom should a person be more grateful than to his parents? The *Sefer Hachinuch* writes that a person must be eternally grateful to his parents because they gave him life, and failure to express gratitude by honoring them is an exceedingly despicable trait.

True, a parent has the right to waive the privileges and honors that are due him from his children, but such a waiver must not be taken lightly. You may feel uncomfortable having your children stand up for you when you come into a room, but did you ever think that it might be good for them?

Many years ago, before I was married, I was present at the *Seder* conducted in the yeshivah dining room by my *Rosh Yeshivah*, Harav Aharon Kotler *zt"l*, the *gadol hador*. According to the Halachah, a *talmid* may not eat and drink in the reclining position when he is in the presence of his *rebbi*, unless the *rebbi* gives him permission.

I was in a dilemma. Should I ask for permission or wait for the *Rosh Yeshivah* to offer it on his own? In the end, I did not have the courage to ask for permission, so I sat throughout the *Seder* without reclining. The *Rosh Yeshivah* said nothing. The second night was a repeat of the first night. Again the *Rosh Yeshivah* said nothing.

This taught me an important lesson. The *Rosh Yeshivah* surely noticed that I was not reclining, and he cared nothing for his own honor and prestige. And yet, he did not offer to give me permission to recline. Why? Because he felt that, at that point, it was better for me sit there in front of my *rebbi* in awe. He felt I would gain much more from honoring my *rebbi* than from sitting in a reclining position.

Don't forget this lesson. Don't be so quick to waive the honor that is due you as a parent. Your children need it more than you do.

There is another area I wanted to touch on with regard to teaching your children values, and that is teaching your children to tell the truth.

There is a certain scene that sticks in my mind from when you were a little girl. I doubt if you remember it, but I do. You came into the living room, carrying an old telephone you must have found somewhere, and you sat down on the couch. It was one of those old rotary phones, and I remember how you concentrated as you dialed some mythical number. Then you started to talk on the telephone. I tell you, if I was in the other room I would have thought there was a real conversation going on.

In your mind at that time, you were experiencing a different reality. You had heard your mother speak on the telephone often, and you knew the cadences. Now you were doing the same thing, and it certainly didn't look like playacting. Do you know why? Because in the child's mind, fiction becomes a reality.

That is why children are such easy liars. When it is convenient for them to tell a lie, they will create that lie in their own reality and actually believe it to be true.

I was once invited to speak at a boys' elementary school. I began by showing the boys two pictures of *gedolim* and asked them to identify them, which they did easily. Then I showed them a picture frame which contained a blank piece of paper, and I asked, "Who is this one?"

The children all looked closely at the blank paper with puzzled looks on their faces. But they said nothing. Finally, one of them summoned the courage and said, "That is no one's picture. It is just a blank paper."

"Now you know what a lie is," I told the children. "A lie is using words to create a nonexistent picture."

This is the job of the parent, to show the child the difference between truth and untruth and to impress on him that a Jew always tells the truth.

You also have to give them a true perspective on the world from the standpoint of strong Jewish values. You have to show them what is good and what is not, what brings people happiness, what is the meaning of success, and you can only do this by example. Your children, who have very keen perception, will see what you hold dear and what you disdain, and they will set their own value system accordingly.

I always like to give as an example the *Seder* night. Ask any child what he remembers about that night, and he will undoubtedly mention the *matzah*, the *marror*, the wine, the *afikomin*, the questions, the songs, the stories.

Do you think for a moment that any child will tell you it was the *matzah* balls in his soup or the fresh potato *kugel* or the delicious brownies?

Why?

Because the priorities in the house on Pesach night are very clear in just about every Jewish home.

On a regular Shabbos, however, it might be a different story. One child may mention the *zemiros* and the *divrei Torah*, while another may speak of the great *cholent* and the scrumptious chocolate cake.

If the parents show enthusiasm and excitement about the exalted spiritual experience of Shabbos, the children will focus on that as well. But if the parents view Shabbos as a time to relax and have a good time, the children will miss out on the holiness and beauty of Shabbos.

The bottom line is that it all depends on the parents.

The Importance of Teamwork

Dear Daughter,

Last but far from least, I want to discuss with you the most critical factor in bringing up your children. But first — did you guess? that's right — I want to tell you one of my little stories.

Some time ago, a couple asked my advice about certain choices they had to make for the education of their child. They were at the point of choosing a kindergarten for their child, and they were in a dilemma. Should they choose a Yiddish-speaking kindergarten which would give him a valuable tool for learning in later life? Or should they go the more conventional route and choose an English-speaking kindergarten, since English was the language spoken in their home?

As they discussed the question, something became very clear to me. Instead of objectively analyzing the question, there was a struggle going on between husband and wife, a struggle characterized by tensions and stubbornness. It was very disturbing.

"Let me explain something to you," I said. "The question of Yiddish or English is supposedly for the good of your child. You both want to make the choice that will assure his success in school. Well, let me tell you what is even more important for his success. Teamwork! The two of you have to be a team working together in harmony for his good. That is the most important element of all. If your child senses any argument or disagreement between the two of you, it will have a very counterproductive effect on his performance in school."

I saw that my words were having an effect on them.

"Think about this," I continued. "A child from a poor home visits a rich home where he sees such beautiful things and so many conveniences. Then he is asked if he wants to go home or stay there. What will he say?"

"He will want to go home," said the wife.

"Why?"

"What do you mean why?" she said. "That is where he lives. That is where his parents are."

"Exactly," I said. "Because all those things are nice, but they don't give him life. His home and his parents give him life. They are him. When parents work together as a team, this solid authority that comes from deep love and harmony becomes part of the child. In the same way that he would never consider leaving his home, he would also never consider rebelling against this benevolent, precious authority. But if he senses disharmony between his parents, he will instinctively try to manipulate them. And let me tell you, children are very good at manipulating parents. Then you're in trouble. Do you understand what I'm saying?"

They both nodded. I could see that I had opened their eyes.

"My advice to you is to go home and work together on becoming a team. If you're a team your child will be successful even if he has to learn in Chinese. When you feel you've really come together, then we can discuss relatively minor details such as Yiddish versus English."

There is a Midrash about a king who entrusted his beloved son to a famous pedagogue. After a few days, the king summoned the pedagogue and asked him, "Did my son come to school on time? Did he leave on time? Did he eat? Did he drink? Did he sleep?"

Do you notice something strange about this Midrash? I'm sure you do. The king asks all these question, but not the most important one, the one that addresses the reason the prince was entrusted to the pedagogue in the first place. The king should have asked, "Did my son learn?" But he didn't. Why not?

The Alter of Kelm explains that the Midrash is teaching us a very important lesson in chinuch. If a child is ill prepared to learn, the best pedagogue in the world will not be successful with him. If he is hungry, thirsty, overtired, he will not learn. But if he is well fed and well rested, it is not even necessary to ask if he learned. Of course, he did.

As important as it is for the children to eat and sleep in order to be able to learn, it is equally important for them to enjoy a positive home environment. Tension in the home is very disruptive to learning, but where there is peace and harmony, the children thrive.

If you and your husband are a true team, if you approach the issues in your home and the upbringing of your children in a spirit of peace and cooperation, your children will undoubtedly be successful.

And so will you.

This volume is part of
THE ARTSCROLL SERIES®
an ongoing project of
translations, commentaries and expositions
on Scripture, Mishnah, Talmud, Halachah,
liturgy, history, the classic Rabbinic writings,
biographies and thought.

For a brochure of current publications
visit your local Hebrew bookseller
or contact the publisher:

Mesorah Publications, ltd.
4401 Second Avenue
Brooklyn, New York 11232
(718) 921-9000